ELEMENTS OF
RESEARCH

A Guide For Writers

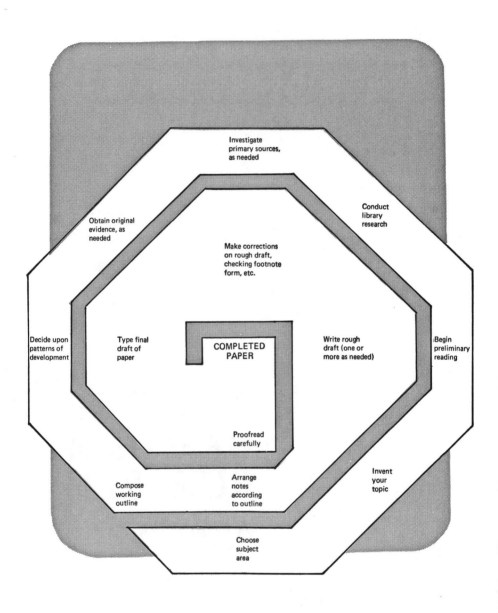

ELEMENTS OF
RESEARCH
A Guide For Writers

**CAROL T. WILLIAMS
&
GARY K. WOLFE**

Roosevelt University—Chicago, Illinois

 ALFRED PUBLISHING CO., INC.

Library of Congress Cataloging in Publication Data

Williams, Carol T.
Elements of research.

Includes index.
1. Report writing. 2. Research. I. Wolfe, Gary K.,
joint author. II. Title.
LB2369.W48   808'.042   78-12170
ISBN 0-88284-070-3

To Kary and Joe,
and Joey, Megan, and Christopher

CONTENTS

Chapter Two (continued)

Chapter Three: Primary Source and Original Evidence Research

Chapter 4: Development

Chapter Five: Research Form

Chapter Five (continued)

PREFACE

In 1978, about 55 percent of the Gross National Product of the United States was in some way a product of information processing. With the various kinds of information storage and retrieval playing such an increasingly vital role in our lives, knowledge of how to gather and use information skillfully is rapidly becoming one of the necessary survival skills of an educated person. One of the premises of *Elements of Research: A Guidebook for Writers* is that these skills are every bit as important in the "real" world—the world of business, politics, government, community involvement, even recreation—as they are in the college and university. Knowing how to think creatively about professional and personal problems and knowing where to look for solutions are often the same skills needed to produce an academic research paper. Thus, while the immediate focus of this book is how to conceive and write an effective academic research paper, in a broader sense this is a text on *problem solving*, on learning what we need and want to know, and on gathering and presenting this information in any context.

Because of this emphasis on the practical value of research skills, we stress a number of areas that until a few years ago might have seemed unusual in a college course in basic research techniques. We devote an entire chapter to "invention," the process of moving from a general idea of what to write about to a specific problem. In another chapter, we recognize the increasing importance of primary sources and original evidence. Although primary sources and original evidence-gathering techniques are often taught at the graduate level in specialized disciplines such as sociology, psychology, and economics, we feel there are good reasons for emphasizing them in an introductory research text. One is the increasing need to use primary sources and original evidence in undergraduate classes in subjects where scholarship is still young, such as media studies, popular culture, regional studies, or environmental studies. Another is that educated adults must often face problems in their life or work situations that require the "detective skills" of working with primary sources and generating original evidence. A third practical emphasis in the book is a chapter on problems of development, or organizing and "subduing" masses of researched material into a coherent paper. How to do this is a complex problem that goes far beyond the arrangement of note cards; we treat it as a rhetorical problem of choosing the most effective arrangement of material for any extended paper or report.

In the more traditional sections of the book, Chapter 2 on library research and Chapter 5 on footnote and bibliography form, we retain emphasis on the practical by exploring issues such as the kinds of libraries students and writers are likely to use, the most efficient way to use time while in a library, variations in footnote and bibliography form, and forms for such relatively new kinds of citations as movies or television programs. Basic to these chapters are diagrams on procedures and forms, which serve as convenient reference tools.

Throughout the book, then, we try to establish a link between academic research skills taught in college classes and problem-solving skills required of everyday life. The organization of the book, as a whole as well as in its parts, is intended to reflect the logical, step-by-step nature of a practical skills manual—or, as our subtitle indicates, a "guidebook."

The ability to locate and manipulate information has become a survival skill in a society in which information processing of one sort or another has become the major income-producing activity. But the ability to research is more than a survival skill. It is a way to exert power and control over the masses of data that surround us, a way to become more comfortable in a world of information, a way to learn what we need to learn when we need to learn it, and thus to become less dependent on formal educational experiences and better able to make education a lifelong activity. Beyond that, research can be rewarding for its own sake, by helping us clarify our thinking on all issues, feel less threatened by the problems that confront us, and simply enjoy the excitement of being able to explore ideas with some confidence and grace.

This book began as a module, or independent study unit, written in 1975 for Roosevelt University's External Degree Program. Since then, we and several of our colleagues have used the module in teaching our classes and independent study students. Thus, our primary acknowledgment must be to our students, who were our first, and remain our best, critics. We wish especially to acknowledge the work done by Virginia Fry, an artist and a student of the module, whose revisions of the module are deeply imbedded in our Chapter 1. We are also grateful to Joe Williams, whose ideas on invention underlie our system of analysis in Chapter 1; to Kary Wolfe, for her ideas as well as her editing and copyreading skills; to Pat Novick, for her sociologist's help on the section on questionnaire design; to our editor and friend, Emmett Dingley; and to our typist, Roberta Fireman.

1

What to Write About

How can you decide what to write about? Whether you are assigned a general topic for research or have the world to choose from, the problem is the same. First, start with what you have—curiosity, knowledge, and the ability to think logically. Curiosity leads you to questions, knowledge helps you answer questions and shows you what more you need to learn, and logic orders your knowledge in a reasonable manner. Let's apply these basics to the task at hand.

INVENTING

Invention is discernment, choice.

—Henri Poincaré

The process of moving from a general idea to a specific topic is called *invention*. The term was once commonly used to refer to any literary or artistic composition (many musical works are called "inventions").[1] Our system of invention is similar to developing writing skills in general, especially the skills of "argument" and "developing a topic," because a research paper is, above all, an act of writing.

---

[1]The most famous classical work on the subject is probably *De Inventione* (*Of Invention*) by the Roman orator, Cicero.

THE THREE ELEMENTS:
PURPOSE, SUBJECT, AUDIENCE

The three basic elements in any writing process are purpose, subject, and audience. Inventing is discovering the creative relationship of these three elements. The process of invention is asking questions of yourself about what effect you want to have on your audience and what aspects of your subject will best achieve this purpose.

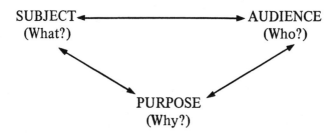

SUBJECT ←——————————→ AUDIENCE
(What?)   (Who?)

PURPOSE
(Why?)

This model shows the three elements of the invention process, subject, audience, and purpose, and their dynamic relationships to each other. The arrows represent the connecting questions: How are all three related? How does one affect the other? Since the three elements are interdependent, you can start with any one. But generally people have an idea of a subject area, so we will begin our questions there.

For example, you may want to write about the great—or awful—movie you just saw. Then you have to ask what is your purpose in writing; that is, what effect do you want to achieve? The answer will determine your audience. Do you merely want to clarify your impressions of the movie? Then write only to yourself (in a diary, let us say). Or do you want to communicate with other moviegoers, in hopes of persuading them to see, or not to see, this particular film? You may want to address a specific critic who has already reviewed it, and with whom you disagree. Do you want to communicate only with that critic (write a letter), or do you want to use your criticism rhetorically, to persuade a larger audience, (write an article or essay)? You can see how one question leads to another, and how each decision you make regarding your audience and purpose will modify your subject and the way you present it.

THE TWO GENERAL PURPOSES:
TO INFORM; TO CONVINCE

Of course, everything you write is in some sense an attempt to convince your audience, if only of the reliability of your information. However, purposes generally are of two types: primarily to inform or primarily to convince your audience of the soundness of your position. But remember that here we are talking about purposes, not about your mode of development, or rhetoric (which we will discuss in Chapter 4). Your most powerful rhetoric might be information, even though your purpose is not merely to inform, but to convince.

To choose which lines of development will be the most effective for your purposes, you must consider who your audience is. A useful analysis of an audience depends on the ability to empathize, or "get inside their heads." You cannot hope to know what kinds of arguments will convince an audience, or even what kinds of information they will need in order to feel informed, unless you discover what they know and value, and what they don't know, disdain, or dismiss.

Let us take a currently controversial example: the dissemination of birth control devices to minors without parental knowledge. If your purpose is to persuade a parents' group of the physician's right to distribute birth control devices, you would lose before you start if you ignored the parents' feelings and argued for individual rights as you would to a group of disinterested civil libertarians. Or, suppose you wanted to inform and convince an audience of the social value of computers. What chance would you have with an audience of lay people if you used the technical terms appropriate for an audience of people in the computer field? Obviously none! You would convey no information and would antagonize your frustrated readers to boot. Nor could you convince a group of technicians that their computers were a threat to your privacy, if you failed to empathize with their dependence on the machines for jobs and with the faith they may have in their product. In analyzing your audience, you should first consider viewpoint—yours and your audience's—and then vocabulary—yours and theirs.

DISCOVERING YOUR SUBJECT:
A SYSTEM OF "QUESTIONS"

Here is a system that will help you invent your subject. The system is a series of questions for analyzing subjects, discovering possibilities that may not have occurred to you, and organizing those that have.[2] Basic advice to writers usually goes as follows: choose a subject that interests you enough so that you can make it interesting to your audience, that you can find sufficient information on, and that is neither too broad nor too limited to fill the requirements of the paper. But where do you go from there?

Let us first look at this system of analysis in general, and then in more detail. Remember, as you ask and answer these questions about your subject, that the idea behind them is to stimulate your thinking so that you will be able to develop the subject in the most creative way. Let your mind wander to new areas suggested by your exploration. The process is virtually open-ended—you could probably spend a semester inventing the subject *restaurants*, for example. You can't explore every possibility you think of; but if you plan on about a two-hour session for analysis and the weeding-out and pruning process that should follow, you may well find that you have your paper virtually outlined, and also that the subject is far more exciting than you imagined when you first, tentatively thought of it.

Is your subject a whole or part of a larger system? With any subject, any experience or idea, you can move from your first, tentative thought essentially in two ways. You can look at the subject *internally,* as a self-contained and independent entity. Or you can look at it *externally,* as a part of a larger entity or related to other entities in a parallel manner. For example, the city you live in can be studied in and for itself, and it can be studied in relation to other American cities or larger governmental units, such as state and federal.

How do you examine your subject as a state and as a process? Whether you treat your subject as a whole or as part of a larger system, you will discover more possibilities if you examine your subject both as a *state*—a static, complete-in-itself entity—and as a *process,* a dynamic, changing flow. Again, a city can be seen as an

---

[2]This system is based on Joseph M. Williams, *The New English: Structure, Form, Style* (New York: The Free Press, 1970), pp. 160–193.

entity, a body of people, land, institutions, and so on, and also as a seemingly infinite arrangement of processes, from garbage collecting to the activities of the Board of Trade.

What is the relationship among parts of a subject? Each subject can be analyzed into its functioning parts, and these parts can be classified into relationships of environment and dependency. For example, the subject of a television news show could be analyzed into parts such as news, weather and sports; or reporters, producers, writers; or substance, style, setting. The parts could then be classified according to their *environmental* relationships—weather presented between news and sports, for example—or their *dependency* relationships—the show is dependent on its producer, but also on its sponsor. And if it has a star reporter, such as Walter Cronkite, isn't everyone else—producer, sponsor, cameraman, and so on—dependent on him?

INVENTING "TELEVISION": AN EXAMPLE

To illustrate these terms and their functions further, let's take one subject, television, and examine some of the ways in which it might be invented—how it can be related to larger subjects or to parallel subjects, and how it can be broken down into smaller, more specific subjects. Keep in mind that what we are about to do is not the only way to develop this subject, but merely some possible lines of development.

Because you will be inventing both larger and smaller subjects, you should begin by putting your initial subject in the center of a large sheet of paper:

```
┌─────────────────┐
│  TELEVISION     │
└─────────────────┘
```

Next, think of a way in which this subject may be divided into smaller parts. There are many ways to do this, of course—we could write about the economic, social, and cultural aspects of television; or different historical periods in the development of television; or even the physical parts of a television set. Let's pick for our area of interest the way television is made available to the public. We can think of two major ways: public and commercial broadcasting. So beneath the word TELEVISION we write these subtopics:

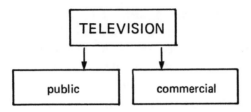

Suppose now that we are most interested in commercial broadcasting. We can further subdivide this topic, since there are at least two ways that commercial broadcasting is made available: through networks and through local stations. So we divide the subtopic "commercial television" thus:

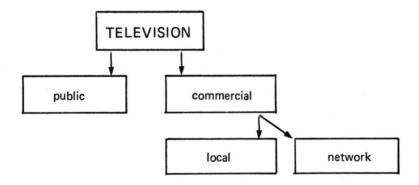

Now let us pursue network broadcasting. We could subdivide this topic in a number of ways: according to the functions of those who work on network TV (sponsors, creators, network management), or the network organizations (ABC, CBS, NBC), or the types of programs offered. (Can you think of other ways to subdivide the topic of commercial network television?)

Suppose we choose types of programs, distinguishing between entertainment and news programs. Our chart now looks like this:

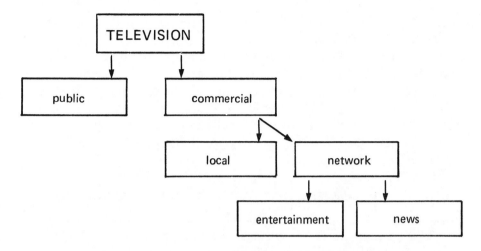

If we are most interested in entertainment programming, we can subdivide that topic, say, into dramatic programs, sports programs, and music-variety programs. And if we choose to explore "dramatic programs," further subdivisions emerge: soap operas, comedies, and dramas, for example. We could go on subdividing almost endlessly—dividing dramas into police shows, family dramas, and so forth; then dividing police shows into those starring men and those starring women, and so on. But let's pause and look at our chart so far:

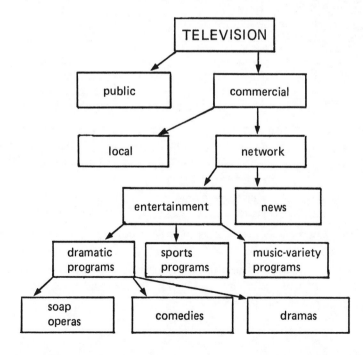

Perhaps we want to stop now and write our paper, say, on the characteristics and development of television soap operas. But let's not stop. If we invent in some other directions, we may turn up a more interesting subject, or we may be able to see interesting relationships between soap operas and other subjects, either larger or parallel. For example, of what larger topic might "television" be a subtopic? To explore this, we must build our chart above the central subject TELEVISION, listing as many possibilities as we can think of. It might look like this:

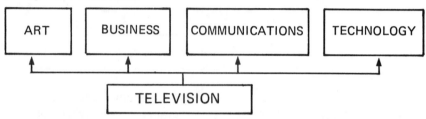

Let's say that we find television as an art most interesting. But what is art a smaller part of? Well, it is part of culture. Are we going to deal with television in all cultures or just our own? Are we going to treat the entire thirty-year history of television in our culture? More inclusive topics begin to appear above the middle of the page:

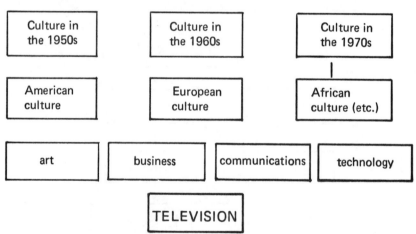

We have not drawn connecting lines in this upper portion of the chart, because we want to show that there are alternative relationships among levels of topics; for example, television → communications → European culture → in the 1970s; or television → art → American culture → in the 1950s.

Still, we have not exhausted the possibilities. When we look at these larger topics of which television is a part, we begin to think of other topics that are also part of each larger topic—in other words, topics to which "television" is parallel. Under the larger topic of "art," for example, there are other arts to which television might be compared, such as movies, novels, and plays. (Similarly, we might think of other businesses to which television might be compared, or other communications media, or other forms of technology.)

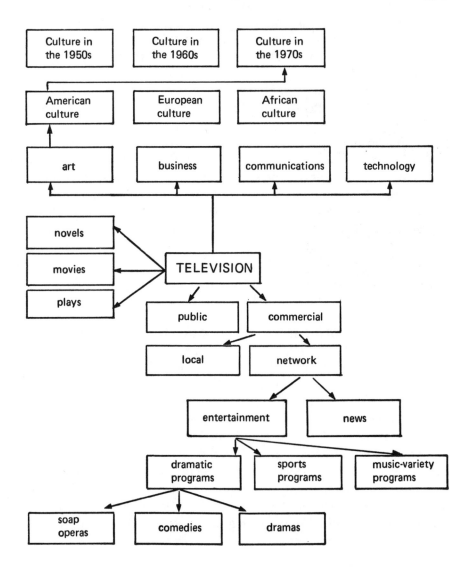

On our chart, we will place these similar topics parallel to "television." At this point our chart is still not complete—an invention chart never is—but by now we have developed "television" to the point where many possible research topics emerge. The chart now looks like the one on page 9 (with one alternative arrangement illustrated in the upper portion).

As you can see, the chart does not show all possible topics that could be derived from "television," as for each level of topics that we generated we have selected only one topic for further development. When you use this method of inventing a subject, you will find that you select and discard topics as you go along. The chances are that among those that are left will be exactly the topic you want to write about.

INVENTING "RESTAURANTS": THE THREE QUESTIONS

In the preceding section we examined one aspect of the invention process—determining the parts of a subject—using television as an example. Here we will use the system of questions to invent in detail the subject "restaurants." Remember, the questions are: (1) What are the external and internal parts of your subject? (2) How are they related according to dependency and environment? (3) How do they exist as states and processes?

Internal Structure: Analysis by Parts

Let us begin by looking at the internal structure of our subject. *What are the elements, or functional parts, of a restaurant?* There is equipment, such as stoves, tables, bars, which is arranged in types of areas, cooking, dining, office, and so on. These parts are arranged in environmental, or spatial, relationships to each other. But there are other, experiential parts of a restaurant, such as decor, cuisine, cleanliness, and service, that can be analyzed as well as its sinks and stoves. Looking at environmental relationships may stir provocative questions about their effects on the experiential aspects of a restaurant. What, for example, is the effect on efficiency if the cooking area is in the middle of the dining room? (In some cases, such as homey, "ethnic" restaurants, it may be good; in other, more formal dining rooms, it would probably be a disaster.)

You can also ask questions about the dependency relationships of experiential arrangements. What is the effect on the atmosphere, tone, or "ambience" of the restaurant if the bar is in the dining area? What if it is a piano bar? And what if it is a piano bar with a small dance floor? Or, what is the effect if the quality of the food is subordinate to decor, ambience, and piano bars?

It may also be productive to look at the relationships among parts in terms of outside dependencies. For example, kitchens are dependent on subparts such as stoves, but they are also dependent on outside purveyors such as meat and produce vendors and gas and electric companies. Don't be concerned if this line of questioning about outside dependencies seems to be taking you to external relationships. Television can be perceived as a part of the larger subject, technology, or it can be broken down into its parts, one of which is *its* technology. Similarly, restaurants can be seen as a part of the city's culture, or they can be analyzed for their "culture," or ambience.

Internal Structure: Classification

The next potentially productive kind of questioning is how the subject can be analyzed by class and types or subsets of a class. The subject "restaurants" can be classified by cost, with subsets such as cheap, moderately priced, and expensive restaurants; it may be classified by ownership (individually owned or franchised restaurants); or ethnicity (Japanese restaurants, French restaurants) and so on. You may choose the class, single restaurant, classifying it as to service, food, atmosphere, and other subsets. Classification might lead to a statement of purpose or thesis statement for a term paper along the lines of, "The food at Chez Guido is mediocre, but the service and imaginative decor are so far above average, one almost forgets and forgives."

When you begin to organize a subject into its subsets, even a subject as relatively simple as restaurants, you quickly discover that the helpful exercise of classifying raises as many questions as it answers. Subsets can proliferate; one can classify almost any subject almost infinitely. Types overlap; and classifying breeds bias—ignoring the particular, atypical instance. You should make special note of the "exceptions to the rule" that you discover as you invent your unruly subject, for one of them may make the most interesting subject. So not only does classification enable us to put likes together with likes, we can also use classification to pinpoint "unalikes." Suppose we want to find out whether ownership is a factor in restaurant quality. We try out a subset, franchise-owned versus individual or family-owned restaurants, and we conclude on the basis of our evidence that the franchise-owned restaurants generally offer poorer food. But we found one franchised restaurant that offers good food, it is then pinpointed as the exception, possibly worth the focus in a paper.

Internal Structure: The Subject as Process

All of the restaurant-classification possibilities that we have described (kitchen, dining room; Japanese, French, and so forth), were conceived of as states—entities that exist in space. You can also analyze and classify your subject as it exists in time, in terms of its ongoing process. The same classification procedure can be followed, but this time you will look at the types of processes and their smaller phases.

You may decide to write about the history of restaurants—a long process or change over time; or the changing ownership of a particular restaurant—a shorter process that is part of the larger process of the restaurant's history; or a particular change of ownership—a process which is a still smaller part, or phase, of these larger and longer processes.

Process refers not only to history but to any sequence of actions in which your subject is involved. If you inquire into the procedure by which the owner manages the restaurant, you are looking into a process. If you ask how the food is prepared, the answers will describe a process.

You will also want to explore the way the various processes are related by dependency. Your questions may turn up sequences of actions that look like cause-effect relationships. What caused this restaurant to change its location? What are the effects of its moving out on the neighborhood it left? On the neighborhood it moved to? In order to establish cause and effect you have to ask about intention. What were the owners' reasons for moving, and what do they hope to accomplish by the move? Keep in mind that reasons are not the same as causes. Don't assume that the reason the restaurant moved is that the old neighborhood is "deteriorating," even if you have heard the owners state this opinion. It may be that the two processes—the restaurant's move and the neighborhood's change—are not dependent on one another. The owners might not have moved had they not received an attractive offer for their old building and an attractive deal on a new site. Processes may also be related by *antecedents*—first A happens, then B, followed by C—or they may be coincidental—occurring at the same time—but in both cases the events are not causative. Suppose that the restaurant in its new location is hit by a string of fires of mysterious origin. The cause could be arson—but it could also be defective wiring, careless employees, or some other logical cause. The fires could even be accidental, or (most complicated, and probably most normal of all), a combination of any or all of the above.

Two Kinds of Processes: Past or Current

If the process you are examining has already happened, you want to look at it as a whole; that is, as a sequence of actions with a beginning, middle, and end. If the process is ongoing, you cannot define its incomplete phases conclusively, but you can predict, based on historical precedent and logic (and, if you think you can carry it off, personal authority). In fact, predicting the end of currently active processes (elections, "changing neighborhoods," or other social processes) is one of the commonest purposes in writing.

You might predict that the restaurant will do better in its new location than it did at the former site. You might cite historical precedent—your research discovered that related businesses have done well when they located in that neighborhood recently. You might cite a neighborhood need for a restaurant of that particular type, say a moderately priced Japanese restaurant, if you classified the types already located there and found there were no Japanese restaurants and if you surveyed the neighborhood residents and discovered they would be interested in patronizing the new restaurant. Other reasons for predicting success—or failure—are also possible. If you select an ongoing process as a subject for a research paper, be sure you make your reasons credible by presenting evidence of the sort we suggested here—surveys, historical precedent, and the like.

External Structure: Classification and Analysis

The questions you used to analyze and classify your subject as a self-contained state or process can also be applied to exploring your subject as part of another or larger state or process. Simply reverse your perspective: how does your subject function as a subset of larger sets or classes or in relation to other, parallel subjects. Look at the states and processes you have already defined, and try to see them as related parts and types of larger or parallel states and processes. For instance, looking externally at the relocation of your particular restaurant, is the change a part of a general trend of shifting businesses? Is it part of an overall process of population change, and if so, how does it fit into the new pattern that is emerging?

Don't let your imagination fall into a rut of commonplace associations. Restaurants are a subset of "businesses," and businesses are a subset of the "American economy," and so on. But suppose you find your interest in restaurants comes from an interest in commercial architecture. Then you might view your subject as a type or subset of the class "commercial buildings." Or suppose your interest is popular culture—you might want to compare the ambience of new and old restaurants or different ethnic restaurants. Or you may be interested in a social subject, such as "the ways Americans entertain themselves," or "the class consciousness of Americans." Restaurants are a potentially interesting subset of either of these larger classes or subjects. You might begin your paper as follows: "We can learn a lot about the class consciousness of Americans by looking carefully at the places they choose to 'dine out.' " Be careful to demonstrate a significant relationship between your subject and the larger set of objects, experiences, and ideas. Even when you are sure that such a relationship exists, keep in mind that the relationship is not absolute—choice of a restaurant is also determined by other factors than class consciousness.

In analyzing how your subject functions as a state in relation to other states, again look at environment and dependency. What are the various environments of which your subject is a subordinate or coordinate part? What are the restaurant's relationships to other businesses, types of commercial architecture, ways of entertaining ourselves? What is its relationship to its neighborhood, or to its period in history? And on what larger elements is your subject dependent?

Does your restaurant depend on a citywide transit system? On neighborhood police protection? On the other hand, in what ways are larger subjects dependent on yours? Does the city's tourism or the "spirit" of a neighborhood depend on its restaurants? "Turning a question around" is one of the most stimulating invention techniques.

External Structure: Processes

Your subject is now a phase of a larger process, but the method of analysis is the same as for internal structure. Examine causes logically. Are they necessary, sufficient, or only contributory to the effects? Are they in fact causes or only antecedents, with no relationship to later stages in the process other than that the events occurred in sequence? What intentions have motivated the process?

Can you see the larger process as a whole, with a beginning, middle, and end? What are your predictions if it is an ongoing process? What other processes is it like? Did the beginning, middle, and end of restaurants in the neighborhood coincide with the rise and fall of its commercial life in general? If so, is this process part of a larger one, such as "deterioration of the neighborhood because 'undesirables' are moving in"? Or is it part of the process, "deterioration of a neighborhood because businesses are moving out to the suburbs"?

Note the word *because* in the last two statements of processes. Is it *necessary* that businesses move to the suburbs, or that "undesirables" move in, for a neighborhood to deteriorate? Are such events *sufficient* by themselves to cause a community to decline? Or are these *contributory* causes? If so, what are the other contributors? When you begin to examine the conditions necessary for labelling events as causes, you can see how careful you have to be. If you call a mere antecedent a cause, or call a contributory cause sufficient for the effect, or if you omit some causes, you will open a large hole in your argument.

INVENTING YOUR SUBJECT: CONCLUSION

Now you should be ready to use the system of questions to generate the subject and direction of your own paper. Take a large sheet of paper and *diagram* all the possible topics that can be derived from a single idea, as we did with the subject "television." First put the subject in the middle of the page; then expand it internally by working down the page, branching from larger to smaller topics, and externally, by working upwards from the subject as a subset of increasingly larger classes and processes. Don't forget to work sideways, testing other, seemingly parallel, subjects. You may choose first to break down an idea into parts, think up parallels, or see an idea as part of larger relationships. The important thing is to think in all three directions before you settle on your topic.

To get a reasonably expansive and satisfactory overview of your subject and its possibilities, use the system of questions to analyze and classify your subject. You will use lots of paper, testing lines of inquiry and making notes on promising topics (and being sure to note any exceptions you find when classifying, since they may be your most important and original discoveries). Inevitably, you will expand your initial subject beyond what is practical for a single research paper, but eventually you will find on your chart a manageable topic.

When you get far enough along in your inventing to have a bulk of notes and a healthy "tree" branching out from your subject, go back over the topic possibilities and *choose* those that interest you most and show particular promise for development. These will be the topics and lines of development with which you will begin your library research. As you choose some possibilities and eliminate others, examine their relationships to each other. For example, you may decide to write a paper about how the coming of a restaurant contributed to the decline of the neighborhood. Thus you plan to eliminate as a subtopic the internal parts of the restaurant (kitchen, dining room, and so on). But before you do this, ask if these parts may have contributed to the restaurant's bad effect on the neighborhood? Perhaps the bar attracted undesirable persons into the community. Or maybe the kitchen was too small, causing trash to spill out onto the street. Choose your points for development carefully— but be even more careful in eliminating topics.

In selecting a topic for further investigation and development, keep in mind the *purpose* of your paper, the *audience* for whom it is intended, and the topic's *researchability* (or how you will go about finding information). Purpose and audience come first: if you can't think of any good reason for presenting this topic to your prospective audience, there is no point in worrying about how to research it.

For each subtopic you propose to investigate (and for any subtopics you are not sure of the value of), take a few minutes to answer these two questions:

1. What would be the purpose of including a discussion of this topic in your paper?

2. How might this topic help the audience in understanding your purpose, and how might they react to it?

The answers will help you further to define your topic and establish some priorities for your first trip to the library. For example, if your paper is going to be on Henry Ford's contributions to manufacturing techniques, one possible subtopic might be the early life of Henry Ford. But what would be the purpose of including a discussion of Ford's early life in a paper principally concerned with methods of manufacturing? Is such information necessary or helpful to your audience, or might it be merely distracting and annoying? If you decide that your purpose and audience do not warrant such information, then you have saved yourself some work later on.

As you question the purpose and audience of each subtopic you will find that the remaining subtopics become more closely related and your ideas about your subject more thoroughly developed. Your notes about purpose and audience will begin to repeat themselves; this is a good sign, since it will help you in the final step of invention—deriving a *central theme* and purpose that is especially geared to your specific subject and audience. When a central idea emerges, you will know how to conduct your research, both in and out of the library, and how to construct your paper. You will have spent a couple of mentally taxing hours, and you will be surrounded by what seems like a ream of paper filled with notes, crossed-out, rewritten, and perhaps coffee-stained; you may even feel that you have eliminated most of your subject, although each of those eliminations has actually helped you to sharpen and focus your subject as it relates to your purpose and audience. But you will also be involved in your subject in a way that may surprise you, and you may even discover that you have, in effect, a working outline for your paper—and a clear sense of what you need to find when you begin your library research.

PRELIMINARY RESEARCH QUESTIONS

Now that your topic is invented, you are almost ready to begin preliminary research. But before you do, you may find it helpful to make some decisions about this topic that can make your research easier.

How much of the topic needs research? No matter how good your topic is, you may not be able to *prove* your point at all! Many of the most important problems cannot be solved through research alone; we can never "prove" that war is evil, since there are so many different ideas of what evil is, and since these ideas rest upon fundamental articles of faith rather than on factual evidence.

What kind of research will the topic need? In deciding what aspects of your topic can best benefit from research, keep in mind that every topic involves at least one of three kinds of problems. At various times your topic will probably touch on all three.

KINDS OF PROBLEMS

Logical problems.   Some problems may be solved through simple logic; that is, the solution is hidden in the problem itself, and the answer is not likely to be found through research (though a method for working the problem might be). Mathematical problems belong in this category. If you want to find out what 356 x 79 is, you wouldn't go to the library in the vague hope of finding that particular problem worked out in a book, nor would you take a vote to find out what most people think about this issue. You would simply work it out according to the logical processes of multiplication. Nor would you need to research the proposition that someday you will die, since logic tells you that you are a member of a group in which all members are mortal.

Empirical problems. *Empirical* means capable of being tested against experience, and a wholly empirical problem is one that can be solved through research alone. "What is the capital of Albania?" is a problem to be solved by consulting an up-to-date reference book. No amount of logic alone will give you the answer, and no amount of belief that the answer is really Detroit will change the observable facts.

Those aspects of your topic that need information to be supported are the empirical aspects of the topic, and they are also the aspects you will probably want to focus on in your research. Chapters 2 and 3 are principally concerned with empirical research; that is, with finding needed information.

Moral problems. Some aspects of your topic may reflect moral beliefs. Even if such a belief is at the very heart of your paper, you will probably not be able to "prove" it in the strictest sense. What you must do is clearly distinguish the moral issues in your topic. Many of the breakdowns in communication over such issues as capital punishment and abortion arise because people try to provide empirical or logical proofs of an issue that depends upon moral assumptions. Since so many contemporary topics do involve moral issues, let us look briefly at the problems involved in conducting research that rests on beliefs in addition to provable facts.

"RESEARCHING" BELIEFS

There is no formula for persuading an audience of the correctness of a point of view. But you can learn to effectively present the moral issues of a topic through research that (1) considers the past (history or tradition), (2) considers the majority, and (3) objectively assesses your own credibility as a personal authority.

The fact that an idea has endured over time is an argument in its favor. What it means is that many people have experienced the idea as valuable or worthwhile and we may learn from their experience. This is probably not a conclusive argument, and after investigating it, you may decide the idea is no longer valid—that times *have* changed—but the argument from tradition should not be spurned as old-fogeyism.

Secondly, consider the majority: "Fifty million Frenchmen can't be wrong." Of course, fifty million Frenchmen (or Americans) may be wrong. It may even be, as a character in Ibsen's *An Enemy of the People* says, that "the minority is always right." But if you can understand the majority view, you will be able to present it fairly and objectively. You will be able to write from inside rather than outside the subject. For example, the political designation "conservative" may be anathema to you, but as of April 1975, 62 percent of

Americans called themselves political conservatives. That fact gives you two choices: to dismiss the 62 percent majority as stupid or unenlightened, or to investigate with an open mind. Your investigation may uncover many kinds of conservatives—"rednecks" and reactionaries, yes, but also ecologists, libertarians, and other conservators of traditional ways and values. When you finish, you may find that some of their beliefs are similar to your own or even that your beliefs have changed somewhat during the course of your investigation. But the important thing is that you will have much more knowledge of your subject and therefore a much greater chance of writing effectively.

The third consideration when writing about beliefs is personal authority. It isn't easy to be authoritative about a belief ("human beings are essentially good," or "human nature can be changed"). But you must take your belief seriously. You probably wouldn't have such a strong feeling if you didn't have some practical involvement, and hence some practical knowledge. What is the nature of that involvement? How credible can you make it; how authoritative? Credibility depends on the subject. For example, who is more authoritative on the subjects of abortion or birth control—the mother or father with experience or the social scientist? The researcher has much to offer, of course. But those who are personally involved also have something to offer, and you should not ignore the authority of their personal experience or your own—just be sure to present it as personal. As teachers we have found that, while some beginning researchers make the mistake of basing an argument almost exclusively on personal experience, others lean too far in the opposite direction. Of course you should research "the experts," but you shouldn't defer to them too easily. Investigate all your evidence critically, empathize with different points of view, and test them against what you yourself know—for unless you use your personal knowledge, you haven't much chance of being creative. And unless you take the chance of being creative, is there really a point in even starting?

TYPES OF RESEARCH

In planning a strategy for your research, it is also productive to consider the kind of research you are engaged in. Essentially, there are four types, though they may overlap.

Original research. In original research the main ideas or their supporting evidence are completely new, and what you are saying hasn't been said before. Although more likely to be done by professionals or graduate students than by undergraduates doing a term paper, it is possible your topic may lead you to do some original research. Of course, original research is based on previous findings; it doesn't spring out of nowhere. And it is largely a matter of emphasis, of the directions you choose for your topic. If you seem to be heading into uncharted waters, then your research is becoming "exploratory"— a term scientist W. I. B. Beveridge uses to describe original research.

Innovative research. A second type of research may be called innovative, or in Beveridge's term, "developmental." It provides a follow-up to established research on a subject, showing how it may be applied in new ways or to new fields. As such, it emphasizes the relationship between the old research and its new potential applications. Showing how a teaching technique developed for primary-grade students can also work well with preschoolers is an example of this kind of research.

Practical research. A third type of research involves the more restricted application of an original concept to a practical problem. If original research demonstrated a need for mental health education for prospective parents, and innovative research showed how this idea relates to child abuse and divorce, practical research might show how such a program could be set up in a particular community.

Borderline research. This is Beveridge's term for the fourth kind of research, which takes place at the border of two or more subjects and uses the subject matter and methodology of all the disciplines involved. This kind of research can be very creative and rewarding but also very demanding, since one must do research in more than one specialized field. A paper that would relate mental health education to such broader issues as behavior modifcation or civil liberties would involve borderline research in law, philosophy, psychology, and education. Scientists call such interaction among areas the "transfer method" in research. Educators call it the "multidisciplinary" or "interdisciplinary" method. The astronomer Carl Sagan found himself working in such an area when his research into the possibility of intelligent life on other planets (*Intelligent Life in the Universe,* 1966) led him to the question of how intelligence evolved in human beings (*The Dragons of Eden,* 1977)—thus moving through several "borders," from astronomy and geology to biology and anthropology. Many contemporary subjects—ecology, sociobiology, popular culture, urban studies, to name a few—invite borderline research.

ATTITUDES TOWARD RESEARCH

What attitude will you take toward your subject? Essentially, there are two attitudes that shape all original writing: affirming and negating. If a writer tries too hard to "play it safe" and walks a tightrope between them, the result is apt to be dull and probably unconsciously biased. Get your biases out in the open. Do you want to refute or correct something that has been said or is widely believed about your subject, or to affirm something new about it? You may, of course, want to do both—first refute other theories and then build your own. This does not mean that you should set out to do a "hatchet job." But in the lively, creative mind, skepticism plays an important part, and the impulse to negate is powerful. In your reading you will come across contradictory evidence; many scholars will disagree over the same evidence. This is how the dialog of creative research is carried out, and you should not be afraid to make your own judgments.

The task of affirming a thesis is much more difficult. If your thesis is a prediction, for example, it will be almost impossible to prove. Affirmation goes beyond criticizing the work of others to marshalling evidence for your thesis and ultimately to stating your conviction based on knowledge and experience. As Charles Darwin, whose own work was built largely upon the work of others, said, "To him who convinces belongs all the credit." But we have already talked of the difficulty of proving beliefs and convictions, and you might well ask if there is any point in trying to convince anyone about subjects that involve faith, or personal experience, or the future.

To affirm a thesis, you will be largely dependent on your ability to think and write clearly and emphatically. You will have to go beyond evidence to persuade readers of what you cannot prove. But a good research paper is more than a mere amassing of facts and figures, and a good writer is not afraid to take a stand when it seems appropriate. Even if you are assigned, for example, to research the question of flexible working hours in business, you will soon find that values are involved as much as facts and figures. The principles of rhetoric, of eloquent, persuasive writing, apply to research papers as much as they do to more personal kinds of writing.

At this point, you have done about as much as you can with your topic before going to the library to do research. By now you should know what your topic is, where research is needed, what kind of research you will be doing, and what your attitude toward your material will be. All of these may change slightly as you move into the next stage of research, but you should also find that your work in the library goes more smoothly now that you have a clear idea of what to look for. In the next chapter, you will have a chance to test your ideas against what is already written on your topic.

2
Research in Libraries

PREPARING FOR RESEARCH

Once you have invented your subject, your next task is, as Samuel Johnson says, to "know what books have treated of it"—and what articles, monographs, lectures, essays, films, television programs, pamphlets, and recordings. Any research project involves dealing with a huge amount of material, not all of which will make its way into the final paper or report. What material you decide to use will depend on your estimate of its value for developing your topic. In any event, your material must be found and organized before you start presenting conclusions in the form of a paper or report.

TYPES OF EVIDENCE:
SUFFICIENT VERSUS INSUFFICIENT

As biologist W. I. B. Beveridge has written in *The Art of Scientific Investigation*, "Probably the main characteristic of the trained thinker is that he does not jump to conclusions on insufficient evidence as the untrained man is inclined to do." What constitutes sufficient evidence will vary according to the level of research you are engaged in and the audience to whom this research is addressed. There is a difference between sufficient evidence that you discover in research and sufficient evidence as presented in your final paper; you may become convinced of something by all the evidence you have encountered in your research, but unless you present this evidence in a clear and persuasive manner in your paper, your audience is not likely to be convinced. You need not present *all* your evidence in your paper, however, since in many cases this will be impractical. Try to keep as your standard the idea that sufficient evidence is that which would convince an objective observer who hasn't done all the research you have.

Evidence is sufficient by virtue of its quality as well as its quantity. Two or three sources that seem to support your point will not be convincing if evidence is widely available that argues against that point. To give an extreme (and silly) example, it would be possible to do a research paper that argues that the earth is flat, and to support this argument with the authority of some of the greatest of ancient philosophers. But almost anyone could immediately see that such an argument fails to account for the astronomy research of the past three centuries.

TYPES OF EVIDENCE: PRIMARY AND SECONDARY RESEARCH

Research is generally of two kinds, *primary* and *secondary*. Some exploration in both kinds of research is usually necessary to investigate almost any topic, but the distinction between the two is not a hard and fast one. Primary sources consist of things like letters, manuscripts, eyewitness accounts, diaries, maps, charts, works of fiction, your own observations—anything that might be considered "raw" or uninterpreted data. Secondary sources are works that interpret the information they present; this includes most scholarly books and articles and reference works. But whether a work is primary or secondary for your particular purposes depends to a large degree on the topic you are working on. For example, if you were doing a report on welfare fraud that used newspaper accounts of specific cases to support your points, the paper would be a secondary source. But if the focus of your argument was on how the media presents welfare fraud—if, perhaps, you were arguing that newspapers report only dramatic or exceptional cases and ignore the broader issues—the same newspaper accounts would be primary sources. In the latter case, the newspaper itself is part of your topic; in the former, your topic concerns something you have learned about *through* the newspapers.

Both kinds of research are important. You can't do a meaningful critical research paper on a Hemingway novel without reading that novel (primary research) and then looking to see what others have written about it (secondary research). An elaborately researched paper proving that traffic at a particular intersection is dangerous without traffic signals may be debunked quickly by a critic who points out that you neglected the primary research of observing the intersection and noting that in fact the traffic signals were installed last week.

This chapter and the next will help you discover and evaluate both types of sources for your research. Now you are ready to do the preliminary research that will help you to focus and develop your topic creatively. The preliminary research will also enable you to evaluate your topic better, and perhaps to modify or even discard it in order to follow a more fruitful avenue of research. For this reason, some preliminary reading is almost always necessary before you launch into the more detailed processes of research, and certainly before you undertake primary research. Needless to say, the logical place to begin preliminary reading is the library.

TYPES OF LIBRARIES

Let's explore what you might expect to find in each of four kinds of libraries you might use: the relatively small regional or neighborhood public library, the larger urban public library, the university or college library, and the special interest or research library.

The Small Regional or Neighborhood Library

Learn as much as you can about your own local library. They are often more convenient than other kinds, and once you are out of college they may turn out to be your primary source of research information. Small public libraries are not designed for doing extensive research, of course, but most of them will contain at least a number of standard reference works, some recent magazines, and a substantial number of nonfiction books. In addition, many now feature collections of records, pamphlets, and even films for use by their patrons. But their book collections are likely to emphasize fiction rather than nonfiction, and popular books rather than scholarly books. For this reason, you should not assume that the books on a given topic that happen to be in your local library will provide you with the last word on a subject. But you can begin the process of research, at least by consulting basic references such as encyclopedias, *The Reader's Guide to Periodical Literature* (see page 40), dictionaries, and a few bibliographies. The notes you take from these sources may then give you a clearer idea of what to look up when you get to a larger library, and save you time in the process. And since these libraries are small and have a smaller public to serve, it may sometimes be easier to find a recent book here than in a larger library, since there may be less demand for it and less time needed to process it.

Many small libraries—perhaps most suburban libraries—increase the number of books available to their patrons by participating in an *interlibrary loan* system with other libraries. Interlibrary loan works quite simply: When your local library doesn't have a book that you need, it sends in a request to the system to find the book. If any other library in the system has a copy of the book, it will send it to your library, where you may check it out. This may mean a delay of a couple of weeks, but if you start your research early enough, it can be a convenience. If a book you need is not listed in the card catalog of your library, ask the librarian if it is possible to request it through such a system. As in larger libraries, if a book you need is in the card catalog but is checked out, you can *recall* or *reserve* it and you will be notified when it arrives.

The Larger Urban Public Library

If you live in or near an urban area, it is a good idea to familiarize yourself with the major public library in your area by finding out how you may go about obtaining books from it, what special collections it has, and how extensive its research facilities are. While many urban libraries are designed principally to provide books for leisure reading, some, such as the New York Public Library, are also major research institutions.

A large public library has many features in common with the smaller regional or neighborhood libraries—and, indeed, neighborhood libraries in many cities are often branches of a larger central library. Unlike the smaller library, however, it is apt to have a fairly large collection of reference works and it is more suited to research, since its collection of nonfiction is large enough to include a number of scholarly works, special collections, and city newspapers. But it may still lack the specialized works of scholarship and the scholarly periodicals that are necessary for research in most academic fields.

University and Research Libraries

This is the sort of library that most instructors have in mind when they ask you to do library research. The most accessible of such libraries, is your own college library. Although much if not all of what you need may be available here, your college library may also participate in an interlibrary loan program; some colleges even enter cooperative library programs that allow you to use the libraries at universities other than your own—but often only if the books and periodicals you need are not available through your own college library. Consult your college librarian about such systems.

Know your own college's facilities. How good any library is depends partly on how well you know how to use it, and your college library is designed especially for your use. This means that most of the books and periodicals are ordered in consultation with the faculty, to assure that the collections adequately support the teaching and research that goes on at your college. Furthermore, the librarians have experience in assisting their college students with research problems. Your instructor may rightfully assume that this is the library you should be most familiar with—and keep in mind that this is probably the library your instructor is most familiar with.

The Special Interest Library

In addition to university and public libraries, there may be in your area a number of private and public reference libraries with specialized holdings that you may consult. Usually, these libraries are for reference only and do not circulate books. They are maintained by various research organizations, museums, businesses, government agencies, and societies, and include books of special interest to people involved in these organizations. Many of them, however, will allow a writer such as yourself to consult their holdings if your research requires it. There are libraries maintained by professional organizations such as legal, medical, dental, psychological, and engineering groups; municipal reference libraries that include local ordinances, minutes of city council debates, and the like; and historical societies, which may include more detailed holdings and special collections on a narrow geographical region than larger libraries are likely to have. To get an idea of which special interest libraries may be located in your area, ask the reference librarian at your college— or look up "libraries" in the yellow pages of your phone book.

LOCATION AND TYPES OF LIBRARY MATERIALS

Know the layout of the library you are planning to do your work in, and plan your research so that you can do most of the work necessary in one part of the library before moving on to the next part; this can save you endless scurryings back and forth between rooms. Each type of material has its own location in the library. Here is a listing of the parts of the library and the materials they contain:

1. The card catalog, which consists of files containing cards listing the library's holdings.

2. The reference room, where you may find encyclopedias and standard reference works such as handbooks and yearbooks; bibliographies; and periodical indexes.

3. The periodicals room, where magazines, journals, and newspapers are kept.

4. The stacks, or general book collection.

You might also find it helpful to learn where coin-operated copying machines, typewriters, coin-changers, and such labor-saving devices are located—and the restroom! The simplest way is to ask a librarian. In fact, it is a good general rule to get in the habit of asking librarians for help when you are lost or at a dead end. Most librarians are extremely helpful, and while you shouldn't expect a librarian to do your research for you, shyness in asking for help only wastes your valuable time.

THREE STAGES OF RESEARCH

Once your subject is limited to a manageable size, you are ready to go to the library and prepare a working bibliography to help you get started. This is simply a list of book and journal titles gleaned from the card catalog (and perhaps some browsing) that are most likely to give you a good overview of the topic and may lead you to more detailed sources. You should begin your reading with materials from this list.

Essentially, library research may be thought of in three stages or steps: (1) *discovering* what materials will be needed to begin research —that is, learning of the existence of helpful books and articles; (2) *locating* these materials, or finding out where they are and how to obtain them; and (3) *consulting* the materials and, if they are useful, *taking notes.*

These stages seem simple enough, but it is surprising how many beginning researchers try to dive right into stage three without realizing the importance of the first two steps. If you fail to take the time to discover what materials are right for your paper, you may later find that the books you consulted at the outset were not the most useful ones. Many beginning researchers know all too well the sinking feeling that comes when, having thought their research was nearly complete, they come upon a major text or reference work that might have saved them hours or even weeks of research had they consulted it at the outset.

Preliminary research can be done at almost any library, though you will want to move on to larger or more specialized libraries as your research progresses.

DISCOVERING MATERIALS

On the basis of what you already know about the subject (and presumably you learned a little more about it in the process of inventing it), consider the following:

General encyclopedias. Do you feel that your knowledge of your topic is sketchy enough so that you would want to begin by consulting a general information encyclopedia such as the *Encyclopedia Britannica?* If so, include this in your working bibliography.

Specialized encyclopedias and other materials. If you do not need a general encyclopedia, or if you have already consulted one, you may still want to consult the more detailed and scholarly articles in a specialized encyclopedia, such as the *International Encyclopedia of the Social Sciences* or *Van Nostrand's Scientific Encyclopedia.* Familiarize yourself with the major reference books and encyclopedias in your subject area; most of them will be listed in the card catalog under the subject heading and under the subheading "Ref" or "Reference." Or, if you already know the specialized reference books you want to locate, such as handbooks or yearbooks, make a list of specific titles and look in the card catalog under your subject to see if any of them are listed.

The primary value of such encyclopedias and handbooks is in giving you a chance to clarify your own thinking on a topic, define it better, and discover what related topics might be useful in your investigation. You cannot base your entire paper on such sources, since a research paper requires more detailed information than can be found in encyclopedias and the like. The compilers of such books know this, and frequently will provide a bibliography at the end of an article to direct you to more detailed sources.

The card catalog. List all possible headings under which you would expect to find information on your subject in the card catalog. It is important to list as many as you can think of, because sometimes card catalogs play a frustrating game of hide-and-seek with the unwary researcher. Not every heading will be where you expect to find it, and often you will be sent to another heading by a card that simply states "See _____." You might expect to find books on the U.S. Senate under "S" for Senate, but most card catalogs will have books about the Senate filed under "U" for United States—and under the subheading "Congress" and the sub-subheading "Senate." You can see how the process of invention is important in so "simple" a task as finding a subject heading in a card catalog!

Chances are there will be several cards under a given heading; if the subject is fairly broad, there may be dozens or even hundreds of cards for it. If that is the case, you needn't be discouraged, because that means you will be able to use the card catalog itself to help you narrow your topic. Many subject entries are broken down into smaller areas, and within each of these areas you will find books that treat a specific aspect of the overall subject.

If you cannot find your topic as a subject heading, or any of its alternatives, don't hesitate to ask for help. Many libraries that use the Library of Congress cataloging system have displayed for reference near the card catalog a huge book called *Subject Headings,* which will enable you to look up the topic you have chosen and immediately find the corresponding subject heading used by the Library of Congress system.

Bibliographies. Compile a list of bibliographies that might provide useful research sources. You might need to consult a bibliography of bibliographies (such as *A World Bibliography of Bibliographies*) before you can do this. Look under your subject heading in the card catalog to find works that are either bibliographies (indicated by the subheading "Bibliographies" or "Bibl." after the main heading) or that contain bibliographies (this feature of a book will be noted on the catalog card entry for that book, at the bottom). Some libraries themselves compile specialized bibliographies in areas where their holdings are especially strong. Check with a librarian to see if your library has any such bibliographies in your subject area.

Periodical indexes. There are few topics on which you would not want to consult the periodical indexes, which are lists of articles, arranged by topic, that have appeared in magazines and scholarly journals. Most popular magazines are listed in *Reader's Guide to Periodical Literature*; more specialized journals are listed in subject matter indexes such as the *Social Sciences and Humanities Index* or the *Business Periodicals Index* (a list of periodical indexes appears on page 40). To see what periodicals are listed in a particular index, look at the front of the index. Make a list of any *kinds* of periodical indexes (business, social sciences, literature, and so forth) that you feel might be useful for your research (and don't ignore the newspaper indexes such as those for the *New York Times* or the *Wall Street Journal*). It also is helpful to determine the span of time over which you will want to find articles on your topic. The *Readers' Guide* has been published for more than seventy years, but there are few topics for which you would need to read material for *all* seventy years.

You should now have a list of the following: general encyclopedias, specialized encyclopedias, subject headings in the card catalogs, bibliographies, and periodical indexes. Now it is time to locate them.

LOCATING THE MATERIALS

The rest of this chapter is a guide to what to do in the library, and how to use the reference materials we have described.

Using Basic Reference Works

If you have already compiled a list of basic references, the place to begin is in the reference room. The following section, "Using the Card Catalog," describes the procedure for finding reference materials. Let's hope the reference room and card catalog are located near each other; you will probably be making frequent trips between them.

Once you are in the reference room, locate the first of the encyclopedias or other reference works you want to use. Find a seat and prepare to take notes. First find the article you want and scan it—noting only the major topics covered—to see if it's going to be useful. Ask yourself the following questions:

1. Does it present you with new information?

2. Does it subdivide the topic in a way that gives you some ideas about how you might organize your own paper?

3. Does it contain maps, charts, statistics, or illustrations that provide useful information?

4. Does it mention other subjects that may be fruitful for you to investigate for your paper?

5. Does it have a bibliography that may send you to other useful sources?

If you answered yes for (1) or (3), make out a bibliography card (see below) and take notes on the information you hope to use. If you answered yes to only (2) and (4), you don't need to make a bibliography card, but you should make a note of the general subdivisions of the topic and cross-references to related topics for your use in further research. (But if you plan to use a detailed outline of the article for your own paper, you should make a bibliography card and be prepared to credit the source of your outline by a footnote in your paper). If you answered yes only to (5), you don't need to make a bibliography card, but you should note the authors and titles of the books or articles from the bibliography that you want to consult. This will provide you with the beginning of your own preliminary bibliography.

In making bibliography cards, note the information needed to look up the book or article and for possible future use as a footnote or bibliography item in your paper: call numbers, authors, titles, and dates in the case of books; and authors, titles, journal or magazine titles, page and volume numbers, and dates in the case of articles. For footnotes and bibliography add the publisher and place of publication for books. Then all you will need for a complete footnote citation are the page numbers from which you cite material. It will also be helpful, both for your own future reference and in case an interlibrary loan is needed, to make a brief note of the source of your bibliographical information, whether it is an abstract, an index, or a bibliography in a book.

Here is a sample of such a bibliographical notecard:

> Levi-Strauss, Claude. "The Structural Study of Myth," Structural Anthropology. Trans. Claire Jacobson and Brooke Grundfest Schoepf. New York: Basic Books, 1963, Ch. XI.

Now follow the same process for each of the other reference works that you plan to use while in the reference room—scan them for useful information, make notes on the kinds of information, and if appropriate, make a bibliography card for the source.

Using the Card Catalog

The card catalog is your first resource for selecting materials for your specific research needs.

Finding books in the catalog. Catalog cards are of two major kinds: *subject* cards, which list a topic followed by a card for each book on that topic in the library's collection, and which also may refer you to alternative or additional headings; and *book or periodical* cards. Books and some periodicals are cataloged three ways: by author, title, and subject. You will probably use both kinds of catalog cards in your research. Figure 1 is a sample of a catalog card indexed according to subject; the diagram shows what information you may find on a catalog card and the information's uses. (Not all this information will appear on all cards.)

Before you go to the card catalog, find out if you are allowed to go into the *stacks* to pick out your own books, or if you must present a *call slip* at the circulation desk for the books you want. If you can go into the stacks, then call number, author, and title should be all you need to locate the book. If you have to fill out a call slip, it is quicker to copy this information from the card catalog directly onto the slip rather than taking your own notes and later transferring the information to the slip. Call slips are usually available in bins located in the card catalog room, often under the writing tables.

Selecting books from the catalog. Let's assume you now have in front of you the drawer of the card catalog that contains the books related to your subject heading. Make a rough estimate of how many books are listed under this heading. If it looks like there are not enough books, you may have to consult alternate or related subject headings, or perhaps go later to a larger library, or to supplement your evidence with primary research, or even change your topic somewhat. If there is an overabundance of cards, you will have to

Figure 1. Catalog card indexed by subject.

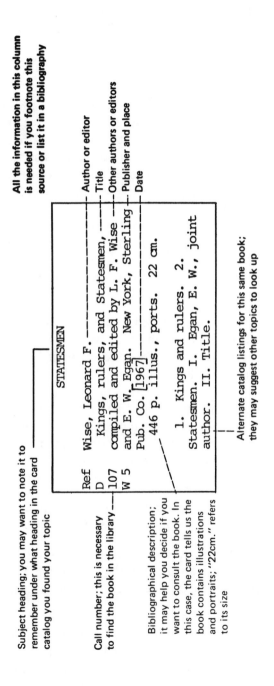

All the information in this column
is needed if you want to footnote this
source or list it in a bibliography

Subject heading: you may want to note it to
remember under what heading in the card
catalog you found your topic

STATESMEN

Ref   Wise, Leonard F. —————————————— Author or editor
D   Kings, rulers, and Statesmen, ———— Title
107   compiled and edited by L. F. Wise —— Other authors or editors
W 5   and E. W. Egan. New York, Sterling —— Publisher and place
          Pub. Co. [1967] ———————————————— Date
          446 p. illus., ports. 22 cm.

             1. Kings and rulers. 2.
          Statesmen. I. Egan, E. W., joint
          author. II. Title.

Call number; this is necessary
to find the book in the library

Bibliographical description;
it may help you decide if you
want to consult the book. In
this case, the card tells us the
book contains illustrations
and portraits; "22cm." refers
to its size

Alternate catalog listings for this same book;
they may suggest other topics to look up

eliminate some based on the particular needs of your own project. The catalog card will often provide you with enough information to discard titles for the following reasons:

- The book is out of date.
- The book is too elementary.
- The book is too advanced or technical (though perhaps you will want to consult it after you have done more basic reading).
- The book treats an aspect of the subject you do not wish to cover.
- The author and publisher information suggests that the book may not be sufficiently authoritative (but you can determine this only if you have some familiarity with the subject gleaned from the reference books you consulted).
- You have already consulted the book, perhaps in the reference room (but check to see if this is a more recent edition than the one you consulted).
- The book contains information that you already have from other sources.

Of the books that do appear to be useful, check to see if you already have bibliography cards for them, from your research in the reference room. If you do, simply add the call number to your bibliography card. If not, make out a bibliographical note card and call slip if necessary.

What books do you want to consult first? As you are preparing cards, make a small note or number indicating how immediately important the book appears to be. One possible system for establishing priorities is to organize the cards as follows:

1. Books that appear to be exactly what you need. This includes books that directly treat your topic, or more comprehensive books likely to include a detailed discussion of the topic.

2. Books that treat the topic, but perhaps in less detail or in a more specialized way than those in the first group. This group might include additional reference works on the topic.

3. Books that contain primary source material—maps, charts, statistics, interviews, fiction, that will provide you with the raw materials needed for your own analysis. Such books might also have information that will help you evaluate the information reported in books in the first two groups.

4. Books that may not treat the subject in any detail or contain any valuable primary sources, but that include useful reference information such as bibliographies. Books that are cataloged under the subheading "Bibliographies" are examples.

5. Periodicals. Except in rare cases (such as monographs), individual articles in periodicals will not be listed in the card catalog, but if a periodical title looks like it may be a journal with useful articles, copy down the title and call number, along with the dates for which the library has the periodical. This can save you a trip back to the card catalog after you have consulted the periodical indexes for articles related to your subject.

Armed with lots of new information from the card catalog, you may decide to do any of the following:

- Go back to the reference room to check out a potentially valuable reference work or two that you missed before.
- Go to the circulation department to get some of the more useful-looking books on the subject. You may want to examine some of these in the library reading room to determine which appear to be worth checking out and taking home for further study.
- Go to the periodicals department to see if you can find information on your subject from magazines and journals. (You will probably want to do this if you have specific references to journal or article titles, or if your topic is so current that there are few books published on it).
- Or you may want to just sit down for a while with the notes you have already made, try to determine what some of the problems are likely to be in further research, and generally rethink your topic.

Using Periodical Indexes, Abstracts, and Microforms

What information is there on your subject in the periodical section of the library? By the time you go to the periodicals, you may have just a few notes from reference books and the card catalog or more extensive notes from other books. But your research will seldom be complete until you have seen what articles in magazines and journals have to say about the subject.

Periodicals are indispensable to thorough research for several reasons. Recent issues contain more current information than can usually be found in books. Many books or parts of books are first published in periodical form, thus making them available sooner, and all the scholarly and professional disciplines depend upon periodicals for up-to-date exchanges of information on current research. Furthermore, if you are interested in finding out what people thought during a particular period (for example, what the trend of military or economic opinion was on the Vietnam war from 1965–1968), periodicals of that time can be your most valuable sources. Finally, a topic too obscure or too temporary to be covered in books may be covered in periodicals.

If you already have some titles of articles you want to read, or titles of journals you would like to browse in, you might want to look those up first. But it is usually a better idea to start with the periodical indexes.

Periodical indexes. Following is a list of some of the indexes and regularly issued periodicals you can consult:

Readers' Guide to Periodical Literature
New York Times Index
Social Sciences and Humanities Index
Business Periodicals Index
Applied Science and Technology Index
Art Index
Education Index
Music Index
MLA International Bibliography (languages, literature, and
    linguistics)
Index to Religious Periodical Literature
Public Affairs Information Service Bulletin
Wall Street Journal Index

Of these, the *Readers' Guide to Periodical Literature* is the one most commonly found in libraries and the most general in nature. Since it comes out about every two weeks, it is also among the most up-to-date of indexes. But it has one major drawback for the scholarly researcher: it lists primarily only general magazines and not the scholarly journals which are more likely to report current research in a specialized field. For this reason, you will probably want to supplement the *Readers' Guide* by also consulting some of the other, more specialized indexes and bibliographies. The librarian will tell you if your library subscribes to an index covering your subject.

Figure 2 is a sample page from the *Readers' Guide,* showing the kind of information contained in each entry, subheadings, and cross-references.

Figure 2. Sample entries from the
Readers' Guide to Periodical Literature.

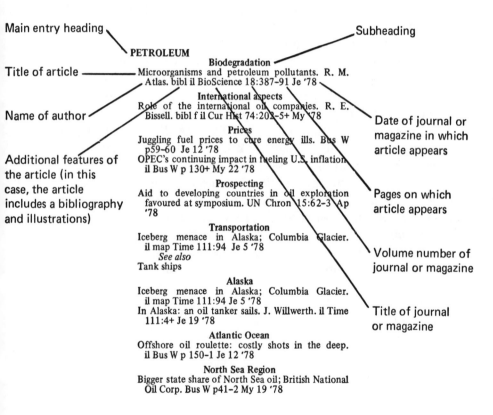

Indexes are like the card catalog in that, if your subject is too broad, they may help you to limit it. Most topics in an index are broken down into subheadings, and many are cross-referenced to other related subjects. You may, then, want to group the articles according to potential usefulness, as you earlier did with books.

Before examining a particular index, you will have to decide how many volumes of the index you need to consult: how far back do you want to go and how recent is the material you need? For example, for articles dealing with President Kennedy's assassination, you would obviously not need to go back further than 1963; while if you were interested in dominant theories of teaching English in the 1950s, you might decide to exclude articles on teaching theory published after 1962 or 1963.

Now you are ready to start work with one volume of a periodical index. Look up your subject heading and see what articles are listed under it. You will probably notice that the articles are cited in what appears to be a sort of code. The periodical titles listed are mysterious publications you have never heard of, like "JASIS" of "AfrSR," and the numbers that follow them look like calculus. Of course, these are merely abbreviations to save space, and the front of the index will give you all the information you need to be able to read an entry, including a list of abbreviations used. (The two examples above are for the *Journal of the American Society for Information Science* and *African Studies Review*.)

When you find an article in the index that looks promising, make out a bibliography card (see page 35) with the following information:

Author
Title of article
Title of periodical
Volume number (if given)
Page numbers
Date

This information is not only necessary to locate the article; it will also be needed should you later decide to cite the article in footnotes or a bibliography. Make sure your bibliography cards are complete. It can be frustrating to be typing your finished paper on the night before it is due and to discover you haven't got all the necessary information about one of your sources. (For details on what information is needed for your footnotes and bibliography, see Chapter 5, pages 130–154.)

If the articles listed in a particular volume of an index don't seem useful, turn to the other volumes of the index you have selected, and perhaps to other indexes. As you become practiced in research, you will be better able to choose which indexes are apt to be more useful than others. If, on the other hand, there seem to be too many articles, it is a good idea anyway to copy down the most promising titles. Some journals may not be available, and some articles you will eliminate after only quickly scanning them. Remember that not everything you consult now has to appear in your final paper as footnotes or bibliography. (The indexes themselves are not listed as references in your paper.) Continue working with the indexes until you begin to get a "feel" for what the scholarship is like on your topic, and until you feel reasonably confident that you have a list of some of the more important articles on this topic.

Abstracts. It often saves time to look up abstracts of articles before reading the articles themselves. Abstracts are brief summaries of the major points of articles, usually written by the author of the article, that will give you a quick idea of whether or not the article is what you are looking for. Abstracts can be particularly helpful if there are a great many articles on your topic, and the titles of the articles as listed in the indexes do not enable you to sort through what is most useful to your research. But keep in mind that not all scholarly articles are abstracted, and that the purpose of an abstract is to lead you to the articles you need, not to replace them. With few exceptions, you should not quote from an abstract when the article itself is available. A few of the regularly issued collections of abstracts are:

Abstracts of English Studies
Biological Abstracts
Book Review Digest
Chemical Abstracts
MLA Abstracts (language, literature, and linguistics)
Psychological Abstracts
Sociological Abstracts
Dissertation Abstracts International (Ph.D. dissertations)

Check with your librarian to see what other abstracts may be available.

Microforms. While you are in the periodical room you may notice that several of the periodicals are stored on microforms—that is, reproduced in reduced size page by page in order to save space, thus requiring special viewing equipment. These periodicals are readily available to you. The oldest and most familiar microform system is *microfilm,* rolls of 35mm film which can be read when passed through a magnifying machine and projected onto the screen of the machine. Less familiar, but gaining wide currency, are *microfiche* and *microcards,* which also require special machines for viewing. Don't hesitate to ask a librarian for help if you need to consult microform materials; the machines are generally easy to operate and rather fun, once you get the hang of them. Many viewing machines now also feature a print-out device, which can provide you with an instant photocopy of the page you are viewing.

Microfilm can be especially important if your research is going to use newspapers, which because of their bulk and frequency of issue are almost always stored in microminiaturized form nowadays. Few newspapers are indexed (though such widely read papers as *The New York Times, The Times of London, The Christian Science Monitor,* and *The Wall Street Journal* are), but if your topic involves news events whose time of occurrence you are reasonably certain of, you can sometimes gather much useful information by scanning the newspapers of that time on microfilm. For example, you don't need an index to tell you that Pearl Harbor was bombed on December 7, 1941. Any newspaper for weeks after that date is likely to have accounts and editorials about the bombing, and such accounts can be among your most valuable primary sources. If you can't remember the exact date of an event (can you remember the exact date of America's first moon landing?), you may want to consult an encyclopedia or yearbook in the reference room to refresh your memory.

If your topic is especially current, clip articles from your own daily papers and neighborhood newspapers (many of which are on file only at their own offices), or take notes from newscasts or TV programs. Remember when taking notes to copy all the information that will be necessary for your footnotes and bibliography, and to write this information on the clippings.

Assessing Your Research to Date

At this point you should have a pretty good notion of how "research-able" your topic is and how long it will take you to collect all the information you need. You have consulted some basic reference works, the card catalog, some indexes and bibliographies, and you may have located and consulted some useful books and articles as a result. Now is the time to plan a schedule of future trips to the library, with specific goals in mind for each trip. How many more periodical indexes will you need to consult? About how long will it take you to look at all the articles and books you have located? What additional research might be needed outside this library? You will, of course, discover still more materials as you begin to follow leads suggested by some of the works you have not consulted yet, so budget "spare" research time, too.

You are now well into the second stage of library research, locating the materials. You may now have to make a judgment about the library you are working in. Does it have enough material to warrant your continuing to work in it, or does it appear that you are going to have to obtain materials from a larger or more specialized library? One way of deciding this is by taking all the bibliography cards for books or periodicals for which you do not already have call numbers and looking these up in the card catalog (bearing in mind that some libraries have a separate card catalog for periodicals). If you find that a substantial number of useful-looking books and periodicals are *not* in your library's holdings, you will probably have to consult another library or use interlibrary loan. If you have several call numbers for books and periodicals but are not sure how useful they are going to be, you may have to consult them before you can decide whether or not to go elsewhere. If there seems to be an abundance of material, you are ready to start reading—although your reading may later lead you to undertake further research outside this library.

Informal Research

As far as formal library research is concerned, you are now well on your way. But there are other, informal types of research, both in and out of the library, that you might want to consider. If your subject is especially current, you might look through the most recent issues of periodicals for information. These would not be indexed yet, but they are probably available in the periodical reading room. If your library has open stacks, you can scan the shelves in the general area of your subject (there may be books you missed in the card catalog that are valuable). Perhaps you might want to look around in some bookstores and newsstands. Very recent books, as well as many paperbacks, often cannot be found in libraries. If your subject deals with an aspect of popular culture—such as television or sports— few libraries are apt to subscribe to the popular magazines that cover it. You might even find useful information just browsing through old magazines of your own or of friends, or in used magazine stores— although this is admittedly a hit-or-miss proposition. If your subject is in an area involving government services, don't hesitate to write, call, or visit the appropriate municipal, state, or federal agency; you may get some primary sources you need (original documents like Congressional reports or your senator's speeches, or facts and figures such as the latest census estimates or the new city budget); and you may get some helpful secondary source material, such as pamphlets on mental health programs, foster child care, or literally thousands of other social and political subjects. The U.S. Government Printing Office alone makes available a remarkable variety of documents at little or no cost. But remember that these pamphlets are usually basic rather than sophisticated or scholarly in content. Using them is like using an encyclopedia; they are only the beginnings of your investigation. Most important, they often are not written by objective scholars or reporters, but by interested parties. With these restrictions in mind, though, you may find them helpful.

Government at all levels produces an enormous variety of both primary and secondary source materials on every conceivable topic, some of which may be available through libraries and some through other sources.

CONSULTING THE MATERIALS

Evaluating Sources: Reliability and Usefulness

Early in your research career, you should develop a habit of critically examining whatever sources you use to determine if they are reliable. Here are some questions to keep in mind about any work you consult in your research:

Does the author appear to be reputable in his or her field? Usually books contain some information about the author—degrees, other publications, and so forth. You can also get some idea of an author's reliability by looking at the text itself and determining if the author seems familiar with other works in the field. Does the book have footnotes or a bibliography? If not, look at the index to see if earlier research is mentioned by author entries. Finally, apply the standards of credible research writing that we discuss throughout this book to the works you are consulting.

Is the publisher reputable? If all the tests of author reliability leave you uncertain as to whether this person is a crackpot or a genius, look at the book's publisher. Most major publishers (such as Random House, Harper & Row, Doubleday, Harcourt Brace Jovanovich, and most university presses) will not risk their reputations by publishing books that have not first been reviewed by other authorities in the field. If a book is published by the author him- or herself, or by a so-called "vanity press" (one that publishes books usually not acceptable elsewhere, with the author paying costs of publication), you should be skeptical of its value for your purpose.

Is the book or article up to date? It would be poor research to cite as your major source a book published fifty years ago, which cannot account for the last half-century of scholarship in your field. Even reputable books by famous authors become dated, and this is even more true of periodical articles. This doesn't mean that you should discount all older books, but where current information is important, use them as supplements to more recent research. Most geology texts prior to fifteen or twenty years ago, for example, would attack and even "disprove" the notion that continents drift, but recent research has led most geologists to accept this not-so-new notion of "plate tectonics." Of course, if you are interested in books as primary sources (see Chapter 3), a book's age is not relevant. Furthermore, older works that are classics of scholarship should not be ignored; these are frequently cited in reference texts or encyclopedia articles on a subject.

The same criteria that apply to books also apply to periodicals. Is the periodical reliable? Look at other articles in the same journal or magazine to get an idea if most of the articles are solidly researched, or if the magazine seems to go after sensational or shallow approaches to topics. What is the editorial stance of the magazine?

Might this affect the reliability of its articles? If you were researching the question of genetic differences in intelligence between blacks and whites, for example, you might well be suspicious of a magazine published under the auspices of the Ku Klux Klan.

In evaluating sources for your paper, you want not only to test their general reliability but also determine if they are useful. A book or article may be a very solid piece of scholarship, well-written by a recognized authority and published by a prestigious publisher, and still not contain the information you need for your paper. Avoid the temptation to "fit" into your paper every book or article you have read simply because you want to show you have read it; this can result in a diffuse and badly organized paper. How well you determine the usefulness of a source is one test of how clearly you have defined your topic. If everything you read while researching seems to have something to say about your topic, that may be evidence it is just too broad to manage. Read the introduction and the index—especially the index which will help you locate useful information and can save you having to read three hundred pages to find the one paragraph you need.

Making Notes

When you go to the library, bring along a good supply of notecards, whatever size is convenient. You may prefer to take preliminary notes in a notebook, but the advantage of cards is that you can conveniently rearrange them later, after you have developed an outline; this will save you from having to flip back and forth among your notes as you move from one section of your paper to the next. We have already described bibliography cards (see page 35). This section will discuss content notes—notes that you will be using as sources of information for the content of your paper. They are of three kinds:

1. *Direct quotations* of relevant material. Such quotations should be painstakingly exact, including punctuation, paragraphing, and even typographical errors in the original (which may be noted by the word *sic* in brackets), and they should be accompanied by the exact page numbers on which the material appears. Use ellipses in place of omitted words from a quotation (see page 123).

Here is a sample of a direct-quotation notecard:

Levi-Strauss, p.
206

In last 20 yrs. anthropology "has increasingly turned from studies in the field of religion"; "all kinds of amateurs ... have seized this opportunity to move in ...."

2. A *paraphrase* of relevant material. This means putting down information from a book in your own words. Note the page numbers of the material you are paraphrasing, and be sure that in writing this material in your own words you are not taking it out of its context or altering its meaning in any way. See pages 118-119 for more detailed information on how to paraphrase correctly.

3. A *comment* of your own that makes a critical evaluation of the source. Again, note all necessary bibliographical information even though your note may read simply "contains valuable bibliography" or even something like "totally useless" (you may later change your mind, of course).

Notes from one source may render notes from another unnecessary, and probably not all your notes will contain information you need for the final paper. All this reading, however, should be a great help in organizing the paper—every source gives you a sample way to organize—and once you have an organization in mind, you will be ready to make an outline. Then you can key your notes to the outline, arrange them in the order of the outline, and be ready to write.

This is a good time to quickly review the stages of library research by looking at the "map" in Figure 3 to make sure you haven't missed any important steps. Keep in mind that this procedure is only one way of approaching library research. You will modify it according to your needs now, and as you gain experience, you will begin to develop techniques and habits that may be better suited to you.

The actual writing of the research paper is the subject of the last two chapters. First we will look at some of the ways you can obtain information that may not be available in libraries of any sort—information you gather from primary sources or original evidence. Such sources are invaluable to any kind of research, and for many topics, they provide the key to its usefulness and interest. Which would you think has the greater potential for being informative and interesting: a paper on nursing homes based entirely on research in libraries, or one which added to this research interviews with patients and staff and some firsthand observations? And which of the two papers sounds more intriguing to write?

Figure 3. A map of library research.

BEFORE GOING TO LIBRARY	Invent your subject (Chapter 1)	Learn layout of library	Learn types of library materials	List likely preliminary sources	Have notecards ready	Go to reference room
IN THE REFERENCE ROOM	Go to card catalog	Check other general references	Take necessary notes →			Consult reference works
AT THE CARD CATALOG	Look up subject	Look up individual books	Determine usefulness of books	Arrange books according to usefulness	Make out call slips	If closed stacks, present call slips to librarian / If open stacks, find books—and browse on shelves around them / Go to periodical room
IN THE PERIODICAL ROOM	Go beyond library	Look through in current issues	Obtain periodicals and take notes	Go to microform room	Consult abstracts	Consult periodical indexes
OUTSIDE THE LIBRARY		Use interlibrary loan	Consult more specialized libraries	Conduct informal research in book stores, etc.	Undertake primary research (Chapter 3)	

3

Primary Source and Original Evidence Research

PRIMARY AND SECONDARY SOURCES

Primary sources—direct sources of information that have not been filtered through the mind of an interpreter—and original evidence—data generated by the researcher—require special skills of interpretation and investigation. In this chapter we will describe primary source material and examine some methods of obtaining original evidence of your own, of discovering facts which may not have been published anywhere.

THE SCOPE OF PRIMARY RESEARCH

Although primary source research is more important in some areas than in others, a certain amount is essential to any paper. When you consult a secondary source on a topic, it is only common sense to compare that source's conclusions and assertions with your own observations of the subject. Even the best authority may make mistakes, and diligent researchers can often discover these mistakes by observation of available primary evidence.

But primary research offers possibilities beyond merely checking the accuracy of your secondary sources. It can be the most rewarding —and sometimes the most expensive and time-consuming—research you will ever undertake. In fact, in recent years, the popular notion of "research" has come to mean primary research, although experienced researchers know that the less glamorous reading and library work involved in secondary research is a necessary underpinning to successful primary research: such reading will tell you what to look for and what questions to ask when you go out seeking facts on your own. The immediate appeal of primary research is the promise of uncovering new and dramatic information, as when Alex Haley traced his family's origins in his bestselling *Roots;* or when reporters Bob Woodward and Carl Bernstein discovered skulduggery at the highest levels of government for the Washington *Post* (and described in their book, *All the President's Men*). However, both Haley and Woodward and Bernstein had time and resources at their disposal. Haley's research began with extensive conversations with older members of his family, first learning the old family stories and legends. Later, when he undertook to find the sources of these stories, he spent years traveling and checking local records in the various states his family had lived in, checking shipping records in America and England, journeying to Africa, and finally—in a rare and dramatic moment that few researchers can hope to duplicate— finding a tribal historian, or *griot,* who could supposedly recite incidents from more than two centuries earlier. Woodward and Bernstein had the advantage of numerous "contacts" in Washington in putting together their Watergate revelations, plus the considerable resources of the newspaper they worked for.

Another recent example of the potential of this kind of research is the work of a librarian named Lawrence David Kusche, who examined the primary sources available concerning the mysteries of the "Bermuda Triangle," a patch of ocean in which ships and planes are reported to have vanished. Bestselling books by several authors had enumerated scores of such mysterious disappearances in that area during the last century or so. Kusche, by consulting shipping records, historical documents, military files, and the like, and by interviewing as many eyewitnesses and participants as he could find, demonstrated that many of the disappearances either never took place at all, took place hundreds of miles from the triangle, or were easily explained by storms, collisions, or simply getting lost. Kusche's diligent research was the result of much painstaking work, but even the beginning researcher can apply his own common sense to a presumed fact. If a source mentions the population of Chicago as standing at 600,000, any Chicagoan can tell from his own knowledge that the source is probably out of date. If a literary scholar gets the name of a character in a novel wrong, anyone who has read the novel closely should be able to detect this error.

When a leading scholar, F. O. Matthiessen, tried to illustrate a point about Herman Melville's use of imagery in the novel *White-Jacket,* he quoted a line that referred to "some inert soiled fish of the sea"—a line that appeared in what was the standard edition of Melville's works. Matthiessen wrote, "Hardly anyone but Melville could have created the shudder that results from calling this frightening vagueness some '*soiled* fish of the sea.' The *discordia concors,* the unexpected linking of the medium of cleanliness with filth, could only have sprung from an imagination that had apprehended the terrors of the deep, of the immaterial deep as well as the physical." But a later scholar, John W. Nichol, merely by consulting the American and English first editions of *White-Jacket,* pointed out that in these editions the word describing the fish was "coiled" rather than "soiled." The replacement of the *c* with an *s* was in all probability no more than a typographical error in the later, "standard edition"! As a result, Matthiessen's use of this particular example sank beneath the waves, so to speak.

Whenever you evaluate a source in the way Nichol did, you are using your own powers of observation as research evidence. *Personal observation, then, is the key to original research*—whether you observe historical evidence directly, by interviewing one or more of the participants in an historical event; whether you observe a literary work or historical document directly, with an eye to drawing your own conclusions; whether you observe a scientific principle by setting up and conducting your own experiments, you are obtaining evidence directly, without the intermediate step of an "authority" on the subject.

There are no sharp lines dividing secondary from primary sources. If you are doing a paper on American history, a book by a particular historian would be a secondary source. But if you are doing a paper on the way history is written about, that same book would be a primary source (writing about historians rather than history is known as "historiography"). And if you personally interview that historian about her methods, you are obtaining original evidence about the writing of history—though this interview would still be a secondary source if your goal is to find out about history itself.

WHEN DO YOU NEED PRIMARY SOURCES?

One of the first questions to ask yourself about your own paper is: are primary sources needed, or is all the necessary material available through secondary sources?

As a general rule, almost any research can benefit from the use of primary sources and original evidence. The more complex and sophisticated research becomes, the more it will depend on such sources. If you confine yourself to secondary sources, you can discuss and evaluate what certain authorities have written about a subject, and perhaps apply their ideas to new areas, but you are not likely to uncover new information about a topic. Such secondary research can often lead to a first-rate paper, and in many college classes, a paper based entirely on secondary sources is acceptable as long as they reveal enough information to allow you to write meaningfully about a topic. Similarly, in business or government work, you may occasionally be called upon to do a summary report of what major authorities have to say about a given topic or problem, and this too can be handled through secondary research. But often you will find that you need to go beyond what "the authorities" say and find information on your own.

How do you know when you need to examine primary sources and generate original evidence? The following questions are a general guide:

- Are there enough secondary sources to provide you with all the information you need to write the paper you want to write?

- Are these sources consistent with the facts, so that you don't need to worry about finding out who is right?

- Do these sources seem sufficiently authoritative; that is, are their conclusions apparently based on adequate primary research of their own?

- Do these sources cover all the relevant facts you will need?

- Does your own experience tend to support what these sources say?

SOME KINDS OF PRIMARY SOURCES

What are some types of evidence? There are literally dozens of kinds of documents that you can use as primary sources; use your imagination in thinking of what the possible primary sources might be for your particular subject. Generally, however, such sources fall into five major categories.

PERSONAL DOCUMENTS

These include diaries, journals, letters, autobiographies, transcripts or tapes of interviews, oral histories, personal essays, addresses or speeches, wills and legacies, notebooks, and memoranda. Often such documents are unpublished and difficult to obtain (although major libraries often have special collections for particular individuals). Some of these materials on major historical figures will be available as published books. Treat them in your footnotes as you would any books, keeping in mind that footnotes or commentary added by an editor would be secondary sources. The *Letters* of James Joyce is thus a primary source, but the "Introduction" to these letters, written by the editor Stuart Gilbert, is a secondary source. Keep in mind also that editing can alter the purity of primary sources. Read carefully the editor's notes on his intentions toward and treatment of the primary material. Here, as so often in primary source research, you must be both detective and judge.

PUBLIC DOCUMENTS

These are the public statements and reports of official governmental agencies or committees, laws and treaties, official proclamations and addresses, constitutions and city charters, records of official proceedings (such as trial transcripts or the *Congressional Record*), judicial decisions and opinions, rules and regulations, and organizational guidelines or charts. Many such documents will include various kinds of charts, graphs, and maps; it is important to know how to get what you need out of them, since they can be intimidating and difficult to read, and they are likely to contain far more information than you need. All public documents are publicly available under law (unless they are classified), but not all are in every library. When looking for public documents in a library, you will find that the "author" is usually listed as the governmental body that produces the document; thus, though Senator B may be primarily responsible for a Committee C's report, that report would be catalogued not under the senator's name, but under "U.S. Government–Senate." If you cannot find the source you need in your library, you may have to contact the Government Printing Office (but try a larger library first).

SEMIPUBLIC DOCUMENTS
AND ORGANIZATION RECORDS

Many organizations, such as corporations, keep records that are produced for the information of employees, members, or shareholders, and thus are widely enough available to be called "semipublic." Examples are annual reports, charters, resolutions, minutes of meetings, position papers, and organizational charts. Relatively few of these are likely to be collected in public libraries (although in some cases, as with professional organizations, the information may be included in a regularly issued journal which is in libraries; look up the name of the organization in the card catalog to see if this is so). To find information not available in libraries, you can go to the organization itself or even check with government regulatory agencies (such as the Federal Trade Commission) to which the organization must regularly report.

CONTEMPORARY HISTORICAL ACCOUNTS

Contemporary, of course, means "at the same time," and if you are researching something that occurred in a particular historical period, you might want to consult accounts written at the same time as the event. Some personal documents will yield this information; the diary of Samuel Pepys remains one of the best contemporary accounts of daily life in London during the Great Plague of 1665. But for more recent history, researchers looking for contemporary accounts would probably first go to newspapers and news magazines. Other sources would include media, such as radio, television, newsreels and documentary films, world almanacs, encyclopedia yearbooks, and books published at the time. In using books, it can sometimes be a tricky matter in distinguishing between whether a book's major value is as a primary or secondary source. Cotton Mather's *Wonders of the Invisible World,* the official report on the Salem witchcraft trials, is a primary source because of its date of publication (1693, contemporary with the trials) and because the author was one of the participants in the event. But Marion Starkey's *The Devil in Massachusetts* (1949), which is also an account of the trials, is a secondary source. In using contemporary accounts of an event, be cautious in evaluating the source, since they are likely to lack historical perspective and often tend to be self-serving. For example, Mather's account of the Salem witchcraft trails in 1693 must be viewed in light of the dominant beliefs of the time and place and the fact that Mather had his own reputation to defend. Wherever possible, then, try to consult more than one contemporary account, and try to corroborate anything you use as a fact in your paper from two or more sources.

WORKS OF ART

If you were researching a particular artist, or a movement, theme, style, or period in the arts, your primary sources would include the art product—novels, poetry, plays, paintings, sculpture, musical compositions or performances (including recordings), films, photographs, and the like. You might also find these sources useful for other kinds of topics as well—as long as you exercise extreme caution in drawing conclusions from them. There exists no more graphic picture of the power of Adolf Hitler than the one in Leni Riefenstahl's film *Triumph of the Will* (1936), and this film is valuable for anyone doing research in that area. But it *is* a work of propaganda, which means the filmmaker was free to exaggerate and dramatize the facts. Her movie is valuable for the overall picture it gives, but it would be an error to cite an episode from the movie as though it were objective fact. Similarly, a portrait of a sixteenth-century king might appear to give evidence that the king was wise and intelligent—but keep in mind that the portraitist may have used artistic license to flatter his subject. With such precautions, however, you may want to allude to and quote from works of art to add color and perspective to your treatment of a topic.

HOW TO INTERPRET PRIMARY SOURCE DATA

It is important to know what a primary source is for a given topic and when to consult such a source. It is equally important to know how to get the facts that you want from it. When you consult a secondary source, you are encountering facts an author has selected to support a point of view. But with primary sources, you must do the selection. The facts seldom fall neatly into place; it is up to you the researcher to know what facts you are looking for and how to draw them out of the mass of material available. For example, if you are using a census report to provide evidence about the increasing average age of college students, you certainly would not need all the information in that report, only that which is helpful to your topic or subtopic. And in relatively few cases is it worthwhile to go plunging directly into primary sources in hope that this will help you define your topic or arrive at a thesis for your paper. Preliminary reading is almost always a necessary first step.

One skill you will need to glean information from primary source material is the ability to read and interpret maps, charts, tables, graphs, and other means of reporting "raw" data. This is a skill that will also aid you in evaluating secondary sources, since many such sources (especially in the sciences and social sciences) incorporate reports of primary research as well as the author's interpretation of that research. By knowing how to evaluate the primary research reported, you can draw your own conclusions and test them against the conclusions presented by the author of the article. Following is a list of some common ways of presenting primary research, with suggestions on how to interpret such data. We will discuss how you might want to use these methods of data presentation in your own paper.

INTERPRETING TABLES

A table is a means of organizing statistical data into several categories in rows or columns. It presents information that would take a great deal of space to present verbally, or information not all of which is relevant to the discussion in the text. A well-constructed table can give you information you need much more quickly than a description in words of the same information. Usually, a table has two dimensions—vertical and horizontal—with one list of characteristics or items along the vertical and another list along the horizontal. As an example, look at Table 1, which shows how Charles Darwin, the great naturalist, organized his observations of species of plants found on the Galapagos Islands (the table is from Darwin's 1845 book, *The Voyage of the Beagle*). There are twenty separate pieces of information in the table, which would take a great deal of space

Table 1
Species of Plants Found on the Galapagos Islands

Name of Island	Total Number of Species	Number of Species Found in Other Parts of the World	Number of Species Confined to the Galapagos Archipelago	Number Confined to the One Island	Number of Species Confined to the Galapagos Archipelago, but Found on More than One Island
James Island	71	33	38	30	8
Albemarle Island	46	18	26	22	4
Chatham Island	32	16	16	12	4
Charles Island	68	39 (or 29, if the probably imported plants be subtracted)	29	21	8

to describe individually, and any single piece of information can be retrieved by simply finding the intersection of a horizontal line entry and the number in a vertical column. For example, if we want to discover how many species of plants Darwin found confined to Chatham Island, we can immediately see that the number is 12, because that number occurs at the interesection of the line "Chatham Island" and the column headed "Number Confined to the One Island."

Table 2 reports the results of a questionnaire given in 1951 to two groups of people, one group opposed to water fluoridation, the other in favor of it. The numbers refer to percentages of the total number of people in a particular group who responded. What percentage of the profluoridation group agreed with the statement that people should not be forced to drink something without their consent?

Table 2
Responses of Pro- and Antifluoridation Proponents

QUESTIONNAIRE ITEMS	Agree		No Opinion		Disagree	
	Pro	Anti	Pro	Anti	Pro	Anti
Scientific bodies like the American Dental Association and the U.S. Public Health Service are the best sources for facts about fluoridation.	92	50	6	15	2	35
A good reason for opposing fluoridation is that it infringes on individual rights.	25	79	12	7	63	14
Fluoridation is *not* a step toward socialized medicine.	65	39	7	19	28	42
Dentists will profit from fluoridation because it mottles (discolors) the teeth.	9	23	18	43	73	34
Since fluorine is only beneficial to children, everybody should not be forced to drink it.	25	85	12	6	63	9
Fluoridation has been a success wherever it has been tried.	45	6	49	37	6	57
Chemical industry is for fluoridation even though it may be dangerous because they will be able to profit from selling their fluoride wastes.	10	52	24	25	66	23
Voting on fluoridation is as sensible as voting on the use of penicillin in treating disease.	61	39	16	16	23	45
People should not be forced to drink something without their consent.	65	93	10	3	25	4
The benefits of fluorine could *not* be obtained by having dentists give it directly to children in the schools.	36	21	32	34	32	45
The water commissioners were taking advantage of their position in starting fluoridation without consulting the public.	31	81	9	6	60	13

(**Source:** "A Study of the Anti-Scientific Attitude," *Scientific American*, Feb. 1955. Authors: Bernard and Judith Mausner. In *Frontiers of Psychological Research*, ed. Cooper-Smith. Permission held by W. M. Freeman & Co.)

INTERPRETING GRAPHS

Graphs may be of three kinds: *line graphs,* in which a continuous line across the page shows changes in values; *bar graphs,* in which bars of differing lengths show comparative values; and *circle graphs* or "pie graphs," in which a circle representing the whole is divided into segments representing the parts. In reading graphs, remember to ask whether the information presented gives a complete and fair picture of the data it represents. For example, the line graph in Figure 4 represents the amount of money invested in pollution

**Figure 4. Investment in pollution control by corporation A
(Jan. 1977–June 1977).**

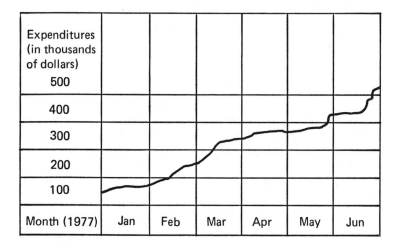

control by a hypothetical corporation over a six-month period. What conclusions are you tempted to draw? It would appear that this corporation is indeed investing increasing amounts of money in pollution control. But the graph does not tell you what the company does in other six-month periods, or how much of the increase is due to court orders or other kinds of pressure, or what a reasonable expenditure might be for a company of this size. Suppose you were to examine Figure 5—which shows the same corporation's expenditures over a longer time period. A lot of questions begin to arise that were not apparent from the first graph. What appears in Figure 4 as a solid trend upward now appears only a minor variation in a six-year decline in Figure 5. What are the reasons for this decline, and why the brief upsurge in expenditures in early 1977, followed by a further decline? These would be questions you would have to investigate further to interpret the data in the graphs.

Figure 5. Investment in pollution control by corporation A (1972–1977).

Line graphs may also be used to compare two or more entities. Had we added a dotted line to Figure 5, representing another corporation's expenditures for pollution, or representing this same corporation's expenditures in another field (such as advertising), a comparison of the two lines would give at a glance some knowledge of how these two values compare over a period of several years.

Bar graphs do not represent as clearly the passage of time, but they can be easier to read, especially where the purpose is to compare and contrast. A bar graph representing the average expenditures on pollution control by three major corporations in three different years might look like Figure 6.

Figure 6. Investment in pollution control by corporations A, B, and C (1973-1977).

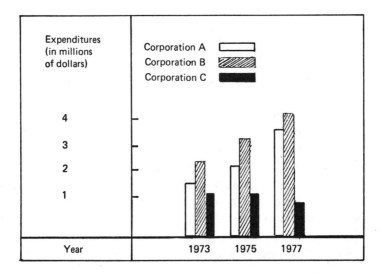

Circle graphs are especially useful for seeing the relative sizes of the parts of a whole, such as how a budget is divided or how a population is constituted. Figure 7 is an example of a circle graph showing how student enrollments are distributed in a university. We can see

Figure 7. Distribution of Student Enrollments in University B.

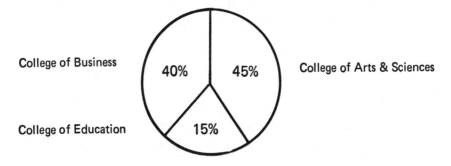

at a glance, without having to add up figures, that nearly half the students in the university are in the College of Arts and Sciences. But while students may register in only one college at the university, they may take classes in more than one. Hence the graph does not give dependable information about student enrollments in particular classes. One of the drawbacks of circle graphs, then, is that they impose rather rigid categories on data. In fact, when you encounter any graph, ask yourself if the categories represented are actually that clear-cut, or if perhaps the graphmaker has simplified the information to represent it more easily.

INTERPRETING DIAGRAMS AND FLOW CHARTS

A diagram is an illustration that shows how something works, or what the relationship of parts is in a whole. You can obtain a great deal of information from a diagram, but only if you read it carefully and do not make easy assumptions about the relationships represented. We are all familiar with the kinds of assembly diagrams that come with model kits or "ready-to-assemble" toys and appliances, and with the trouble we can get into when we think we "know how it's supposed to look" and ignore one part of the diagram. For an example of what a diagram looks like, see the footnote charts on pages 133–136.

   Flow charts represent a process such as how current flows through a circuit, how information flows through a computer, how authority flows in an organization, and so forth. A flow chart may reveal flaws in organization or structure, such as too much authority concentrated in one place, or too many points where error might occur. But again, watch for oversimplification. Does the chart adequately reflect the process as described in the text? Does it take account of all the factors that affect a process? The library map on page 51 is an example of a simple flow chart.

INTERPRETING ILLUSTRATIONS, MAPS, AND PICTURES

In some kinds of research, you may encounter, without any explanatory texts, early sketches by a famous inventor or artist, an old atlas of a region, or old photos or pictures. In order to interpret their significance, if any, you must fall back on your own powers of observation and deduction. By discovering sketches in the notebooks of Leonardo da Vinci, historians determined that the concept of the helicopter was proposed as long ago as the fifteenth century; by consulting old pictures and engravings, costume designers today learn how to create realistic period costumes for plays or movies. By comparing older with more recent maps, scientists can detect subtle changes in coastlines and landscapes, although the scientists must exercise caution, since older maps made without modern equipment can be less reliable. Aside from its scientific value, a map of North America drawn in the seventeenth century tells us a lot about what Europeans *thought* lay beyond the settlements, and that in turn might give us a clearer idea of why they felt further exploration so important.

In looking at old pictures and photographs, first note as many details as you can; use a magnifying glass, if necessary. If you are uncertain of the date of a picture, you can find clues in the kinds of clothing worn, the kinds of transportation used, appliances, apparent energy sources, even fine details such as signs or billboards. Probably none of these will give you an absolute date, but you will be able to narrow the time range. Look also for evidences of posturing or dramatizing: does the picture seem to be candid and realistic, or does it appear to have some artistic or journalistic purpose? A "staged" tableau of a poverty-stricken family is less secure evidence than an unposed sketch or photo of such a family, since the artist making the picture may have distorted the truth for the sake of making a point. If your research subject is an artist or photographer, make a point of examining several works by this individual, noting changes in style and subject matter over a period of time and where possible examining preliminary sketches or "proof" photographs to discover facts about the artist's methods.

HOW TO GATHER AND USE ORIGINAL EVIDENCE

Sometimes research will take you into areas in which primary sources do not yield all the information you need. Or perhaps your research problem is new, and the information does not exist in any form. You will have to discover it on your own. Original research can be the most rewarding kind, since it promises the thrill of "being there first," of finding facts that no one else has found; it can also be hazardous, in that it makes it easy for you to see only what you want to see, and to bias your observations with your own hopes and prejudices.

In some disciplines, notably the natural sciences, the term *research* itself refers solely to obtaining original evidence. When scientists say they are doing research, they usually mean they are setting up and conducting experiments according to the scientific method, not just "reading up" on a subject. But whether you are investigating the biochemical effects of new drugs or writing a term paper on the effects of television viewing, your first task is to find out what has already been done, and only then formulate the purpose for which original research will be needed. It is especially important to have a specific purpose when you set out to obtain original evidence. This does *not* mean having the answers to your questions in mind before you ask them. Rather, it means that if you conduct an interview or survey, you need to know exactly what questions will reveal the information you need to draw reliable conclusions.

In the following pages, we will discuss some common methods of obtaining original evidence. Some of them are similar to the techniques of examining primary sources. The difference is that, in gathering original evidence, you, the researcher, are directing the search for new information.

INTERVIEWS

Interviewing is an attractive method of obtaining original evidence, since there are always people around to be interviewed. But before setting out to interview anyone, find out if (1) the person being interviewed is valuable because of his or her expertise on the subject, or (2) the person being interviewed is valuable because he or she has personal involvement with the subject. If the answer is "no" to both questions, the interview may be of questionable value; your classmates may be easy subjects for interviews, but unless you have determined, for example, that they watch TV for a minimum of three hours a day, the interviews will not be useful for studying the effects of TV viewing. If your answer is "yes" to only one of the questions, that should help decide the sort of questions you would ask.

If the person you are interviewing is personally involved with the subject in a special way, then this person's asides and digressions are likely to be more valuable than those of someone who is being interviewed, say, for a survey. Furthermore, digressions may lead you into new and interesting areas of your subject, and to more specific questions than you had previously thought of. Perhaps you might ask a few general "setting the scene" questions early in the interview; a good practice is to let the person talk with a minimum of interruption, unless he or she begins seriously to stray from the subject. Remember that you are after information from your subject; you are not out to tell this person what *you* think. "Leading" questions that begin with phrases such as "Don't you agree that . . .?" may bias the responses you get. "Helpfully" interpreting your interviewee's answers may do the same. For example:

A: The father seemed dominated by the mother . . . the mother was good. She took care of the child.

Q: She was the stronger character, is that right, would you say that?

A: Yes and no.

Q: Yes and no?

A: Well it all depends on how you mean strong and dominant, but you couldn't say she was a strong person after what she had done.

Q: I was thinking about the fact that they ended up with this kind of spoiled child. Dominant was the word I was thinking of, but overprotecting explains.

A: That's right.[1]

In this example, there is relatively little in the answers that the researcher could legitimately quote in the final paper. The interviewer has almost literally put words into the mouth of the subject, so that the subject confirms the interviewer's thoughts rather than offering original thoughts.

---

[1] In Stephen A. Richardson, Barbara Snell Dohrenwend, and David Klein, *Interviewing: Its Forms and Functions* (New York: Basic Books, 1965), p. 197.

Who to Interview

Of course, the first question you will have about interviewing is, "Who should I interview?" As we mentioned, not all topics lend themselves to interviews. But if you are not sure whether or not your paper would benefit from information gleaned from interviews, consider the following possibilities:

Eyewitnesses or participants who could provide information about a particular event or period. These might include people who participated in strikes, veterans of military actions, survivors of disasters, or people old enough to remember living in your town or working at a particular job at some point in the past. In interviews of this sort, it is especially important not to lead the interviewee, since different eyewitnesses may have different versions of the same event; and not to confine your interviews to a single eyewitness or participant, who can offer only one point of view. Woodward and Bernstein claim that in investigating the Watergate scandal, they made a point of having everything confirmed by two independent sources before they printed it.

Authorities who have studied the topic thoroughly. These could be anyone who has studied a topic enough to be regarded as an expert— scientists, musicians, business executives, artists, politicians, community volunteers, or hobbyists (someone who collects dolls may be able to give you information that would take weeks to uncover through secondary sources). Such authorities, however, must have credentials that you can present to your readers as evidence of their expertise; you cannot treat an eyewitness or observer as an expert simply because he or she "was there." For example, how many who served in Vietnam had any clearer idea of the political philosophies and tactics of that war than most of the rest of us?

Interviewing an authority can be especially helpful if your topic is one on which little has been published, or in which new developments have occurred recently. But be prepared by doing the necessary homework. If an authority has just written a book, and you begin the interview by asking questions that are answered in the book, the authority might well be annoyed that you haven't bothered to read it. Preparation will help you frame pertinent questions and judge the quality of the interviewee's responses.

Creators of works or kinds of works you are studying. If you are doing a paper on an author's work, it can be enhanced by interviews with the author on how a work was written, what it was intended to accomplish, what its sources were, how it fits in with the author's other works, and so on. The same is true of artists, poets, inventors, scientists, systems designers, authors of legislation, architects, or anyone who can be called the creator of material you are writing about. Here again, familiarize yourself with the interviewee's background and other works, and do not try to test your own theories by presenting them to the creator as the "answer." You must be the judge—but you must also uncover the evidence by adroit questioning and sympathetic listening.

Major or representative figures in a controversy or public issue. If there are two or more clearly defined positions on your topic, you might investigate opposing viewpoints by interviewing significant figures who represent them; for example, on the question of tax expenditures for some public program. Such interviews are useful for clarifying issues, but they can be tricky to bring off, since your interviewees must be truly representative of major viewpoints and your questions must be fair to each interviewee. Probably you will have reached some conclusions of your own before interviewing these principle figures, so you will need considerable objectivity to avoid selecting an easy target, or "straw person," to represent a viewpoint you personally oppose, and to avoid asking sympathetic questions of one interviewee while asking trick questions of another.

How to Conduct the Interview

Keep these points in mind while interviewing:

1. Be careful to pace the interview according to a time limit you or the interviewee has set, so that you don't find the interview is over before you have asked your major questions.

2. Research the interviewee as well as the subject. It helps to know in advance if a person is a "hard interview," or shy, impatient, or too talkative. Should your approach be to try,

tactfully, to keep the interviewee on the subject, or should it be to unlock what the interviewee knows by giving him or her a relatively free rein? If you cannot discover these nuances in advance, you can pick them up early in the interview. In other words, try to empathize with the person you are interviewing, to understand his or her position.

3. At the beginning of the interview, explain what you are interested in and what you hope to get from this person—but in general terms and without leading your subject into a corner. If the interviewee asks what your opinion is on the topic, answer honestly, but without suggesting that anything the interviewee might say would be unwelcome.

4. Let your judgment of the person you are interviewing help you decide whether it would be better to begin with specific details and to later move on to broader questions, or to start with the larger issues and later get into specifics. In either case, it is usually a good idea to save any controversial or "touchy" questions for later in the interview after you and the interviewee are more at ease with each other; an inopportune question might bring the interview to an abrupt halt, or cause the interviewee to "clam up."

5. Finally, some details: don't be afraid of silences. Let your interviewee have time to think, especially with complex questions. Don't be afraid to occasionally ask for a clarification of something the interviewee has said (though if you do this too often, you may make your subject feel inarticulate). Don't be afraid to disagree or point up contradictions when you feel such a tactic would stimulate further discussion (but do this tactfully, and in a friendly spirit). Check with your interviewee about taping the interview; a tape recorder can be a convenience, but if it makes the subject uncomfortable, it is better to simply take notes. Even if you do tape the interview, use a notepad to jot down points you want to return to later and information that may reveal attitudes—such as gestures—that wouldn't show up on tape.

SURVEYS

Perhaps you want to discover the opinions, attitudes, or behavior of a large group of people—too many for you to interview individually. In such cases, you may find a *survey* a useful tool. A survey is really a way of conducting many interviews at once, through the use of questionnaires that use standardized questions and answers short enough to be classifiable into groups. The design of surveys and questionnaires is a highly technical skill, and one which you cannot hope to master fully your first time out. But since surveys have become popular in recent years, more and more people are inclined to use them as part of their research. If you choose to conduct a survey, keep the following guidelines in mind.

Who to Survey

The first thing to decide is whose opinions, attitudes, or behavior you want to investigate. Do you want information from the public at large, such as the Gallup or Roper polls usually report, or do you want to investigate a more limited group, such as students or doctors? Next, you must make sure that the respondents to your survey—the people actually answering the questions—represent a fair sample of this group. Ten or fifteen random responses are not a valid means of determining the attitudes of a group that may include thousands of members. If you cannot practically survey a large percentage of the group whose attitudes you want to examine, you must try to achieve a *representative sampling*—a group of respondents who fairly represent the various subgroups of the population you are investigating. Common subgroups might include, depending on your subject, age, sex, income, education level, place of residence, and occupation. If you surveyed only Ph.D. candidates, you could hardly claim that your results represent the attitudes of the group "students," since you haven't included other subgroups of that group, such as high school students or undergraduate college students. The A. C. Nielsen Company, whose representative samples of television viewers have considerable impact on what programs we watch, takes extra care in assuring that the tiny fragment of the American public it surveys represents a statistical approximation of the overall group of television viewers—including all the subgroups we mentioned above.

Similar precautions are taken by major opinion research organizations such as Gallup and Roper. Although you will not have the resources or statistical expertise of these organizations, when you undertake a survey you must nevertheless keep their example in mind.

Types of Surveys

The checklist, or "closed-ended" survey. This is a survey in which your questionnaire includes the answers from which you want your respondents to choose. This method is most convenient when surveying large groups, but it may give distorted information if the checklist is not well designed. A congressman once surveyed his constituents with the yes-or-no question, "Do you feel that Russian aggression in the Middle East is a threat to world peace?" giving the respondents no choice but to agree that there *was* Russian aggression in the Middle East. The value of the data you get from a survey such as this lies in numbers; that is, it will emerge only as you compile the questionnaire responses; and begin to draw conclusions. For this reason it is important that you ask for responses that are easily measurable or "quantifiable"—questions that can be conveniently tallied, such as yes-no or multiple-choice questions. "What is your opinion about national health insurance?" would not belong in this type of questionnaire—as you would quickly discover once you began to tally the almost infinite variety of responses you might get to such a question.

The short-answer, or "open-ended" survey. This gives your respondents more leeway, since they can write their own answers rather than choosing among those you have provided. It is important in a short-answer survey to make sure that the questions can in fact be answered briefly, and that you don't ask people to summarize in a word or phrase their thoughts on complex issues. Such surveys lack the advantage of being easy to summarize that the checklist offers, but may make up for it in providing you with useful sample quotations and giving you a greater range of response upon which to base conclusions. But avoid trying to turn such questionnaires into mini-interviews, with too many follow-up questions embedded in the same question. For example:

Do you feel that proposals to build permanent colonies in space are viable? Why or why not? If so, should they be financed with tax money, at the expense of social welfare programs? Explain.

Although such questions may be familiar to you from essay examinations in college, they are likely to be intimidating and annoying to someone who is merely taking the time to answer a questionnaire for no reward. In the above question, there are two simple yes-no questions that could be part of a much simpler checklist. If a more detailed response is what you want, the question might be rephrased in a more direct manner:

Briefly describe your attitude toward proposals to build permanent colonies in space with regard to (a) their viability, and (b) means of financing them.

Note that the phrase, "at the expense of social welfare programs," has been omitted. Such a qualification sets up a dilemma for your respondent, who might not agree that such programs would have to be reduced to pay for the colonies.

The long-answer survey. Here the persons being surveyed have greater freedom to respond with their own ideas, but the responses are less easy to classify than in shorter-answer types of surveys. Unless you are willing to do a lot of work in sifting through and organizing the responses, limit this kind of question to surveys of relatively small samples or groups. However, long-answer surveys can provide you with revealing and insightful material; details may emerge that you hadn't thought of, and that may change your thinking in significant ways. In doing a survey of nursing home care, for example, it could be quite revealing to ask some nursing home residents to write up accounts of their experiences; you may find problems emerging that you would not have thought to ask about in more objective kinds of surveys. Similarly, it can be valuable to get written accounts of a particular historical event in order to compare them and find what they have in common and how they differ. These can also provide you with a good lead-in to a later interview with the author of the account.

How to Construct a Questionnaire

A survey is only as good as the questions it asks, and the questions should be asked in such a way as to get meaningful responses. Here are some points to keep in mind in writing your questionnaire:

Make the responses measurable. Professional surveyors call this "operationalizing" the questionnaire, so that it will elicit answers which indicate the respondents' real attitudes toward a subject, and yet will allow you to effectively measure and compare responses. To do this, you need first to decide what aspects or components of your subject you need to know about, eliminating questions that do not measure anything useful to your purpose. This is especially true of checklist-type surveys, in which pointless questions simply make more work for yourself later on.

Gather necessary personal information. Among the most important variables in any questionnaire are age, sex, occupation, and other characteristics of your sample population. Begin by determining what personal information from your respondents will be important, and in what combination. For example, it may be important to know the age of the respondent, and it may be even more valuable when you correlate it with other personal data, such as educational level. Do adolescents who have only a grade school education feel the same way about federal aid to education as middle-aged people with only a grade school education? It is important also to know what information to eliminate from this part of the questionnaire; a common failing of beginning surveyors is to ask everything they can think of about their respondent in hopes it will all fall into place later. But keep in mind that you have to do the work of tabulating your responses, and that the simple tabulation itself will not inform or persuade many readers. After you tabulate answers, you must interpret them and test for mutual relationships between items.

Avoid "embedded" questions. Don't fall into the same trap as the congressman who asked about Russian aggression in the Middle East; that is, don't unconsciously imply secondary questions in your items. Such "embedded" questions cannot be answered, since they haven't been clearly asked, but the respondent's answers may be seriously affected by them. The question "Do you feel that space colonies built by taxpayers' money are viable?" embeds a question about public versus private support for such colonies, and this embedded question clouds the response to the larger question of whether such colonies are viable at all. If you only want to know about people's attitudes toward space colonies, eliminate the reference to tax money. If, in addition, you want to know about ways of financing space colonies, it might be misleading in your second question to ask only about financing with tax money, since that forces respondents into one of two opposing attitudes; better make this a multiple choice question.

Try to measure behavior.   What people actually do is often more revealing than what they say, and your survey will be more reliable if you can think of questions that reveal attitudes through behavior. If you ask people what their favorite television program is, ask also how often they view it, since they may claim it is their favorite program only to impress you (or themselves!). But don't jump to conclusions about *why* they view it. This is a separate issue, which requires another carefully constructed question or questions. In complex issues involving attitudes and motivations, the interview is the only way to get at what is unique in each respondent.

Avoid dilemmas.   Do not set up "either-or" dilemmas for your respondents. The question "Do you drink more than two eight-ounce glasses of skim milk a day?" gives the respondents only a yes or no choice, and embeds a secondary question as to whether they drink skim milk at all. Think through all possible answers to your question before you write it, then decide what answers are relevant to your purpose, and finally write the question so that respondents can choose a reasonably exact answer. For example:

Do you watch local television news
   a) daily?
   b) several times a week?
   c) weekly?
   d) less than once a week?

Such questions should include all possible relevant answers; but in cases where there are too many possible responses, list only the most common expected responses and add a category such as "Other: explain," though this will give you less easily quantifiable answers.

Use clear language. Remember that every word you write in a questionnaire and its instructions will influence the findings of your survey. Words such as "often," "sometimes," "very," or "moderately" can invite ambiguous answers. Make sure that every one of your words will be clearly understood by your respondents; as Stanley L. Payne points out in *The Art of Asking Questions, electricity* will probably be understood by more people than *watt.*[2] Be aware of the subtle shifts in response that can be created by "little words." Payne gives a good example by showing the differences in responses to a questionnaire about medical costs. According to Payne, 82 percent responded positively to the question, "Do you think anything should be done to make it easier for people to pay doctor or hospital bills?" When the word *could* was substituted for *should,* the percentage dropped to 77 percent, and when *might* was substituted, only 63 percent said yes. As Payne says, the three words "pose [three] different issues." "Should" suggests the "moral issue of need in the sense of 'It's a crying shame! Something *should* be done about it' "; "could" implies possibility (" 'Yes, but *could* anything be done?' "); and "might" implies *probability:* " 'Maybe it could, but it *might* or might *not* be done.' " Payne concludes:

> The results show that more people see the moral need for an easier payment method than grant the possibility of doing anything about it and that even fewer people think such a method is likely to be put into practice. These are three distinct sets of basic content. Yet any one of them might inadvertently have been used alone to cover any or all of the three contents.[3]

TESTS

Tests are similar to surveys in appearance, but different in intent. In a survey you want the thoughts of a person on a particular subject; in a test that person *becomes* the object of your research, or part of it, and the information you are after is information about him

---

[2]Princeton, N.J.: Princeton University Press, 1951, p. 149.
[3]Payne, pp. 8–10.

or her. Tests and measurements is also the subject of a whole academic discipline, and unless you have specific training in this area, it is difficult to set up and administer a test that is valid. If you want to find out what percentage of the population can perform differential calculus, it would be relatively simple to set up a test that would give you this information. But if you wanted to find out if lefthanded people are more creative than righthanded people, you would have to set up a fairly elaborate means of getting a fair sampling of each and administering a generally valid intelligence test (if there is such a thing!) under the proper conditions. If in some cases your research does lead to constructing a test, follow the same general guidelines we gave for surveys in constructing the questions.

OBSERVATION

Interviews, surveys, questionnaires, and tests are all varieties of *controlled observation,* a kind of research in which you make your own observations of phenomena, but within certain defined limits that you have set for yourself. *Uncontrolled* observation is less formal; it simply consists of keeping a sharp eye out for information that may turn up in a given situation. Giving a questionnaire to a group of students is controlled; listening and talking to the same group in the cafeteria is uncontrolled.

The most rigidly controlled observation is one in which you yourself set up the process that is to be observed, either to test an hypothesis or to gain new evidence toward formulating one. Such a controlled process is an *experiment,* and like surveys and tests, it requires specialized knowledge of techniques and procedures. Since techniques and procedures vary widely among the sciences, you should consult more specialized reference books and methodological texts in your subject area before setting up an experiment. This kind of original research is rarely called for in an undergraduate research paper.

There are two ways of classifying observation according to the relationship of the observer to what is observed. You may observe a subject as a *participant,* as a member of the group you are studying; or you may observe as a *nonparticipant,* who is not directly involved in what is being studied. The relationship of observer to observed depends on your topic. It is obviously impossible for you to be a participant-observer in the Civil War, but you may well be a participant-observer if your subject is closer to home, such as management techniques or inflation. It is not always necessary to make use of yourself as a participant, of course; you could do a fine paper on inflation without once mentioning observations from your own experience. Still, if your observations are well-chosen and effectively used, they can lend authority and immediacy to what you are saying. Journalists have often gone to great lengths to gain a "participant's-eye" view of a topic, sometimes having themselves jailed or committed to a mental hospital in order to write an "inside story." Such dramatic measures are of course risky, and may not yield the information you really need; we certainly wouldn't recommend them for a simple research paper!

Some researchers believe it impossible to ever *not* be a participant in your subject. The act of observing itself, they argue, inevitably has an effect on what is being observed, even in a "hard science" such as physics. Nobel-prizewinning physicist Werner Heisenberg postulated the "indeterminacy principle," which (somewhat simplified) states that observations can only get so precise before the very instruments of observation begin to affect what is being observed. In anthropology, Margaret Mead and others pioneered the idea that the most accurate observation of a society occurs when the observer in effect becomes a member of that society for a period of time, minimizing the possibility that the observer's presence will alter the society's behavior.

PRESENTING PRIMARY SOURCES AND ORIGINAL EVIDENCE

Finally, we should devote some space to the formal presentation of original evidence and primary sources in your paper. Primary sources, for the most part, can be footnoted according to the principles laid out in Chapter 5. Original evidence is more complicated, since you may want to present it in the form of visual aids, such as graphs, diagrams, tables, and the like. An experiment can be described in the text, without footnotes, as can uncontrolled observation. But the results of an experiment, the presentation of statistics, geographical facts, principles of organization or detailed processes, or physical structures either require or can often be enhanced by visual aids, which can save thousands of words.

The first principle is to be sure that the visual aids are helpful to the reader and not merely distracting or confusing. Each should include a caption explaining its purpose and how and from whom the information was obtained, and each should be referred to in the text of your paper. It isn't necessary to include a whole page of census statistics in your paper if all you are doing is referring to a single fact from that page. But if you want to describe a population decline in an area over a period of time, a graph might be helpful. Visual aids should never be used to make the paper look more authoritative, or merely for padding.

USING PICTURES AND DIAGRAMS

Simple pictures or illustrations are of value only if they add information that is not in your text or is not clear without them. A photograph of earthquake victims may indeed be "worth a thousand words" in conveying to readers a sense of the devastation wrought by this natural disaster, but if the point of your paper is to summarize recent research in earthquake prediction, the picture adds little. On the other hand, if your paper were demonstrating the inadequacy of a disaster relief program, the same picture might be an invaluable illustration of the weaknesses of this program—*if* it were illustrative in some way of those weaknesses.

A diagram or graphic illustration should also be used only when it can be helpful. A cutaway diagram of the crust of the earth might show how earthquakes occur, but it needs the support of a full explanation in the text. All diagrams should at least be referred to in your text. Flow charts can be especially helpful in illustrating a process, as long as you are careful to include all important stages of the process and all "branches"—points where the process may move in two or more directions.

USING GRAPHS

If your paper is organized chronologically, line graphs can show at a glance the development of a measurable phenomenon; for example, the graphs used to represent month-to-month profits for a business. (For examples of these and other kinds of visual illustrations, see the section on primary sources on pages 63–65.) Bar graphs are good for comparison-contrast papers, if you are dealing with topics that can be quantitively compared. Pie graphs may be most useful in essays of analysis, since they quickly relate parts to a whole.

USING MAPS

Maps are useful if geographical facts play an important part in your paper, or if your paper is organized spatially, such as a paper showing Hitler's conquests in Europe in World War II. They show immediately what the spatial relationship is between two areas, or groups of people, or buildings. Amateur efforts can be completely adequate in showing general relationships, although drawing an original map requires specialized skills.

USING TABLES

Tables are a convenient means of presenting large amounts of statistical information in a limited space, and among the most useful in reporting on any original surveys or tests you may have undertaken. Much information that supports your point but is too extensive to describe in the text can be assigned to a table. Sometimes your data can be presented in either table or graph form. Tables have an advantage in that they require somewhat less skill to prepare than do graphs.

As you begin to do more advanced research in more specialized areas, you will become increasingly sensitive to the appropriate use of visual aids. If we were to regard research as a spectrum, with literary and art criticism at one end and astronomy and physics at the other, we would probably find that visual aids become more important as we move toward the astronomy and physics ends of the spectrum. Generally speaking, in humanities scholarship illustrations are not often necessary; a picture of Shakespeare adds little to a discussion of his sonnets. In the sciences, on the other hand, researchers need to present large amounts of statistical or conceptual information in the form of visuals, simply to save time and space. And in between these two extremes, economics depends heavily on specific kinds of visuals such as graphs, while many kinds of history do not. If your information can be presented clearly without visuals, then forgo them. But if there are many facts that seem to support your point but do not fit conveniently into the flow of your text, visuals may make the difference between inadequate and persuasive evidence. Then you must decide if the visuals are immediately relevant to a particular point within the essay, in which case you would include them within the text; or if they are of more general interest, in which case you would place them in an *appendix* at the end of the paper.

Whenever you use primary sources or original evidence, keep in mind that your paper is primarily a work of *writing,* not of piecing together various charts, graphs, interviews, and the like. Treat this material the same way as material from secondary sources; that is only as raw material you write *from,* not the paper itself. Your task is to find ways to incorporate primary material meaningfully and to maximum effect in an essay that reads as a coherent argument. To do this, you must examine all your material, primary and secondary, and decide how to develop it. This is the subject of the next chapter.

4

Development

Order is a way of arranging units so that they appear to be parts of a developing pattern. The sense of orientation that results from such an arrangement creates a pleasure called understanding.[1]

All writing, including that complex mixture of our own and others' ideas called a research paper, "discovers itself" during the process of expression. As you approach the end of your research, ask yourself, Am I done? Am I ready to write? If you do not have to return to the library, or interview one of your original sources again, or, indeed, develop a whole new line of research, then your answer will be "yes." Now it is time to take your pack of note cards and arrange them in an organization that will help you write the paper you want to write. Remember that your paper should be shaped by your *purpose:* what you want your audience to know and think about your subject. Thus, your next question, as you begin to organize your material, should be, How has my research changed my original subject, purpose, or perhaps even audience? Or, how has it confirmed them?

Thinking through that question should lead you to the next one—the subject of this chapter: How do I organize my material so as to fulfill my purpose? In helping answer that question, we will be expanding on the system of questions for invention, so that

---

[1]Mina P. Shaughnessy, *Errors and Expectations: A Guide for the Teacher of Basic Writing* (New York: Oxford University Press, 1977), pp. 244–245.

patterns of thought we discuss should be familiar mental tracks for you. At the end of the section on development is a summary chart to help you choose the patterns that develop your paper best. But do not feel bound by the arrangements set out here. Use the chart as a *catalog* from which to choose the developmental patterns that meet your needs. Combine patterns, adapt them to your subject, create from them.

ORGANIZATION: GENERAL AND PARTICULAR

Basically, the organization of every research paper is either more-general to more-particular or more-particular to more-general; most commonly it is a pattern of generalizations, then particulars, then further generalizations. An initial generalization supported by specific examples or other evidence and then repeated and amplified is so common because it fulfills every writer's basic purpose: to be clear and convincing.

The following example of a general-particular-general pattern might be a model for beginning a paper. The writer starts with two sentences of generalization about television criticism in America, followed by several quotations (that is, specific examples or evidence) that illustrate his generalizations. This is followed, in the second paragraph by a recasting of the generalizations, but now in the form of a series of questions that introduce the topics of the paper. The last sentence—"These are some of the questions I would like to raise, and begin to answer"—makes it clear what the purpose of these questions is; namely, to ouline the content of the paper.

Television criticism in this country has been regarded with scorn almost from the start. Its practitioners have been called incompetent, superficial, and corrupt not only by media professionals (who might be expected to take offense), but by television critics themselves. In a 1959 survey commissioned by the Fund for the Republic, Patrick McGrady, Jr. wrote: "Television criticism is, by and large, the fitful labor of tired writers of monumental good will, a degree of talent and jaded perspective. As such, its effect is ... generally inconsistent, capricious and of questionable value to anyone." He characterized Jack Gould, TV editor at *The New York Times* until 1971—and the most prolific, most powerful regular television writer this country has ever known—as "the poorest of the major critics ... gratingly insensitive and illogical ... objectionable, whimsical and, perhaps, dangerous." A fellow reviewer (Richard Burgheim of *Time*) once called Gould "a menace as a reporter," a man in need of "vocational guidance." Have our television critics been as bad as these citations assert? Does any one among them, during the years between 1949 and 1974, stand out as distinctive and worth rereading—and if so, for what reasons? What qualities, forms, and standards are common to television criticism? Are there special problems or limitations built into the job which distinguish it from other forms of reviewing? Are there untried or under-used approaches to criticism which might be considered by the observers of American television's second quarter-century? These are some of the questions I would like to raise, and begin to answer.[2]

A note on the question format in paragraph two: you will notice in many of the examples in this chapter, and in your own reading, that phrasing the problem to be explored as a question is a common rhetorical device. It is rhetorical because posing the problem as a question is a subtle way of involving readers in answering those questions. If you wonder about this, try rewriting this paragraph as a series of declarative sentences. It will not only sound duller—less dynamic, more "set"—it will also cast the writer in the role of know-it-all expert, rather than partner-explorer with the reader.

Here is another example of the general-particular-general pattern, a report of a psychological experiment involving our fallible memories. It emphasizes evidence more than generalizations—a model you might want to follow if, as here, the evidence is what is most original or unique in your paper. In the example, the first introductory paragraph and the fourth summary one are equally concise, and the emphasis is on the specific examples in the middle paragraphs.

Repeated tests of forgetting with various groups of subjects in various testing situations have disclosed a pattern that leads to a general theory. To summarize the findings, let us take the performances of a single representative individual.

. . . The subject is given a list to learn in the laboratory for the first time. . . . The subject studies the list until he is just able to repeat it perfectly, and then he is tested 24 hours later. We find that he has forgotten 20 percent of the items. This is a constant rate of forgetting; it holds for all kinds of items and all kinds of student subjects.

---

[2]David Littlejohn, "Thoughts on Television Criticism," in *Television as a Cultural Force* (New York: Praeger Publishers, 1976; published with the Aspen Institute Program on Communications and Society), p. 148.

Next we give the subject a second list to learn and test him on this list 24 hours later. This time his performance is not quite so good as it was in the pure situation; he forgets more than 20 percent. We go on in the same way with a third list, a fourth, a fifth and so on up to 20 lists. . . . We find a startlingly sharp rise in his rate of forgetting. In the case of the 20th list, 24 hours after learning it he has forgotten 80 percent of the items!

The experiment shows that the more lists a subject has learned, the more he forgets of the last list he studied. Somehow, each list learned contributed to the forgetting of the following list or lists.[3]

ORGANIZING THE WHOLE PAPER:
ANALYSIS AND CLASSIFICATION

The principles of analysis and classification that you used in inventing your subject will also help you organize it. Breaking the subject down into its parts, relating these parts by their dependencies and environments, and classifying the parts may generate your essential pattern of development. For example, this chapter, like Chapter 3 on primary sources and original evidence, uses analysis and classification as organizing principles. In this chapter we have broken down and then classified the various modes or patterns of organizing material—including the mode of classification! For another example, here is a concise breakdown of a subject, the "antifluoridation argument."

> A content analysis of the antifluoridation argument shows that it has three main themes: (1) Fluoridation is an experiment which has not proved its value and may hold unknown dangers; (2) fluorides are poisons; (3) treatment by public agencies of the water that everyone must drink is a step in the direction of socialized medicine and an invasion of individual rights.[4]

In this example, analysis consists of breaking down a larger, more general subject into more concrete, specific parts. In addition or instead, you may want to classify your subject as part of a larger

---

[3]Benton J. Underwood, "Forgetting," in *Frontiers of Psychological Research: Readings from "Scientific American,"* ed. Stanley Coopersmith (San Francisco: W. H. Freeman, 1966), pp. 156–157. Originally published in *Scientific American,* March 1964.

[4]Bernard and Judith Mausner, "A Study of the Anti-Scientific Attitude," in *Frontiers of Psychological Research: Readings from "Scientific American,"* ed. Stanley Coopersmith (San Francisco: W. H. Freeman, 1966), p. 295. Originally published in *Scientific American,* February 1955.

subject—that is, to explain it "externally"—moving from the smaller, or more particular, to the larger, more general subject. The title of the article on fluoridation—"A Study of the Anti-Scientific Attitude" —shows how these writers see the "antifluoridation argument" as part of a broader "antiscientific attitude." Analysis shows the parts of a subject, and classification shows how they are related, both turn vague, potentially confusing abstractions into clear, *real* concerns.

The ways of organizing your material described below are mutually reinforcing. You will probably select a dominant mode of organization most suitable to the purposes of your paper and use one or more of the others as support.

QUALITATIVE ORDER

Qualitative order is based on the principle of least-to-most importance. When you are explaining ideas or presenting evidence, a qualitative order is almost essential, as it serves the purpose of simplifying what is complex or convincing the reader that one thing is more important than another. Where either of these is your purpose, you may want to chart a simple-to-complex, or least-to-most important order.

First analyze the order of importance among the parts of your subject. But how do you decide which pieces of information, or which ideas, are more important than others? To a certain extent, you make such decisions every day. When you tell a joke, you know that the most important information is in the "punch line," and you save this information for last. Though formal papers will not have punch lines; they will have information that will be clear only if other information is presented first and information that will have greater dramatic effect if it is presented later. In the following passage, ecologist Barry Commoner first presents information that will be obvious to most of the general public, and saves for later the information that is new in his essay, and which most readers might not think of. (Note again, in the Commoner example, an opening, topic-giving question.)

> For example, what are the true costs of operating a coal-fired power plant in an urban area? The obvious costs—capital outlay, maintenance, operating costs, taxes—are well known. . . . But we have recently discovered that there are other costs and have even begun to put a dollar value upon them.

We now know that a coal-burning power plant produces not only electricity, but also a number of less desirable things: smoke and soot, oxides of sulfur and nitrogen, carbon dioxide, a variety of organic compounds, and dissipated heat. . . . Smoke and soot increase the householder's laundry and cleaning bills; oxides of sulfur increase the cost of building maintenance; for organic pollutants we pay the price—not only in dollars, but in human anguish—of some number of cases of lung cancer.[5]

Of course, you can use a most-to-least-importance order, discussing first that which you want to emphasize. But then, on the principle that what comes last is remembered best, be careful to sum up at the end and state the importance of what you discussed first.

SPATIAL ORDER

Another kind of organization, spatial order, is appropriate if your topic depends in part on geography. Chapter 2, describing a library's facilities, illustrates spatial organization. (It also illustrates our next pattern of development, chronological order, as it leads you step by step through the research process.) Spatial order could apply to only a part of your paper; let us say, to that part of an analysis in which the parts of your subject are broken down according to their physical environment. Or it might be the structure of a whole paper—for example, a paper on the design of a city or a building. (These, incidentally, need not be architectural papers; they might be about any urban-planning problem, such as fire safety in high-rise buildings.) Spatial order is a way of breaking down a topic so that the reader can visualize it. It is a kind of verbal map.

CHRONOLOGICAL ORDER:
HISTORY, BIOGRAPHY, PROCESS

A chronological order is appropriate for describing events in time or life stories. Describing events in time is called historical narrative; life stories are biographies. Chronology is also a natural organization if your intention is to explain a process: how to set up a day care

---

[5] "Salvation: It's Possible," in *Ecology: Point Counter Point* (Lawrence: University of Kansas Press, 1972), p. 229. Originally published in *The Progressive*, April 1970.

center; how the human body wears down; how to invent, research, develop and write a research paper. The chronological pattern emphasizes the conclusion: the cake not the egg, the goal of the revolution rather than its beginnings, the last part of the process more than the earlier phases. So, if you want to emphasize any other point in the time of your subject, you will not want to choose a *purely* chronological pattern. Your paper may, for example, combine the chronological and the least-to-most important principles—as, for example, the "flashback" does in film. Or, as we do in this book, you may balance chronology's emphasis on ends by also emphasizing the importance of some parts of the process, such as invention, by direct statement and description.

CAUSE AND EFFECT ORDER

Chronology is closely related to cause and effect. When you want to show a cause and effect relationship among the parts of your subject, you must arrange a cause(s)-to-effect(s) order for your material (or the reverse: give the effects first and then trace them back to their causes). But first be sure the parts of your subject *are* causally related, and not just related by accidents of timing or chronology (sequence). For example, if you argue that "the cause of all the dissension in today's world is our turning away from Christianity," you may be oversimplifying by making a contributory cause sufficient in itself to create an effect. But is our turning away from Christianity even a contributory cause to "all the dissension . . ."? Perhaps it is only coincidentally related to contemporary dissension; perhaps both dissension and "turning away" are caused by something else.

In order to test causality and to decide which causes or effects to emphasize as more or less important, you should apply the following definitions of, and differences among, the three kinds of causes: necessary, sufficient, and contributory causes.

A *necessary* cause is one that must be present to create an effect. To have a revolution you must have combatants with the will to overthrow established power, and you must have weapons (guns, ideas, and so forth). A *sufficient* cause is one that by itself is able to cause an effect. A *contributory* cause helps, but needs other causes to produce the effect. Very often we confuse the contributory with the sufficient cause. For example, what factor by itself is sufficient to cause a revolution? A tyrant-ruler? The people's will to overthrow him or her? A cache of weapons?

Sufficient causes tend to be negative causes; that is, a dead battery is sufficient by itself to keep a car from starting, as lack of weapons is sufficient to stall a revolution. But neither is *necessarily* the reason why the car or the revolution won't start. There could be any number of other reasons, each of which is sufficient by itself to negate the effect, but not sufficient alone to produce it.

Contributory causes can in combination be a necessary cause. None of the four elements of a research paper—invention, research, development, and form—is sufficient by itself to create an effective paper, but all four are contributory and necessary.

The next step is to find the most convincing mode of presentation—that is, the rhetoric—for your causes and effects. Should you first describe immediate causes or effects or removed ones? Barry Commoner, in the passage quoted above, emphasizes the more removed, hidden costs of coal-fired power plants, such as lung cancer, rather than immediate effects, like the monetary cost of conversion to coal. Rhetorically he is sound in doing this, because the removed effect of cancer probably holds more interest for most of his readers than do the immediate effects of "capital outlay, maintenance, operating costs, taxes."

Here is another example of a removed and quite general cause presented as more strongly related to the effect than more immediate causes. The effect is the automobile tail fin that rose and declined in the 1950s; the cause is the economy and—even broader—the American system of values.

That the tail fin declined shortly after the economic contraction of 1958 is more than simply coincidence. In large measure the rise of the fin can be attributed to a backlash from the deprivations of wartime life. The cars of the postwar era were obvious and ostentatious consumer products which could at once announce a family's economic security and the country's new-found stability, while hiding actual model differences and engineering features beneath pounds of deceptive chrome. Auto styling, and tailfins particularly, were reflections of the prosperous jet age we entered during the decade of the fifties.

By 1960, however, economic considerations altered the purchasing habits of the nation. Compacts had been introduced and styling in general became more austere. In 1959, Ford staff stylist Elwood P. Engel said, "Price is the most important thing on the small car, economy of operation is second and then styling, I would say. The owner is buying transportation and economy, not styling."[6]

Had the writers reversed their order and put first their immediate cause for the decline of the tail fin, "economic contraction," they might have drawn us along on a logical leap to the broader topic, changes in general American values after World War II. But by tackling the more removed relationship first off, they predispose us to see both change in automobile design and economic change as integrated, dependent parts of the subject of changing values. Of course, if their evidence isn't strong, no rhetorical tricks should persuade us "that the tail fin declined shortly after the economic contraction of 1958 is more than simply coincidence."

In both the Commoner example and the one on tail fins, and in general, the more removed cause is the more general. If you are writing up a causal relationship for a general public audience, consider the rhetorical principle that the more general cause should be emphasized because it will interest more of your readers.

COMPARISON AND CONTRAST ORDER

If your paper as a whole is a comparison and contrast, or if comparing or contrasting would serve your purpose in any part of your paper, you should know the two basic comparison/contrast arrangements: (1) presenting one part of your comparison, and then another, and (2) dividing the comparison into parts, or points, and then comparing part to part or point by point. These two arrangements can be summarized as the "all one, then the other" order and the "point-by-point" order. For example:

"All one . . ."	"Point by Point"
American Regions	*American Regions*

I. New England
  A. Economic opportunities
  B. Recreational facilities
  C. Historical value
  (etc.)
	I. Economic opportunities
	  A. New England
	  B. The Southwest
	  (etc.)

[6]Grady Gammage, Jr. and Stephen L. Jones, "Orgasm in Chrome: The Rise and Fall of the Automobile Tailfin," *Journal of Popular Culture*, VIII:1 (Summer 1974), 145.

II. The Southwest
  A. Economic opportunities
  B. Recreational facilities
  C. Historical value
  (etc.)

II. Recreational facilities
  A. New England
  B. The Southwest
  (etc.)

The point-by-point organization should be chosen when the individual points are your central focus. The all one, then the other order, unless you are in tight control, seems to lend itself to valuing the "one" over the "other." For example, if you explore American regions on a point-by-point basis—economic opportunities, then recreational facilities, then historical value—it is easier for your reader to make an objective judgment than it would be if you present the cases for New England, the Southwest, and so on, separately. In a recent book, *Loose Change: Three Women of the Sixties* (1977), the author, Sara Davidson, chose to organize her material chronologically into periods—"California Girls (1943–1963)," "Blowing in the Wind (1963–1965)," and so on. Thus the biographies of her three women (one, herself) are interrupted, and the points in time, such as 1963–1965, emphasized more than the women are. (But her choice was not necessarily the right one—readers more devoted to character than to social history may regret Davidson's choice of organization.)

Let your purpose-subject-audience decide which type of comparison/contrast to use. In the section of Chapter 2 on libraries, for example, we could have chosen to evaluate types of libraries point by point—by numbers of holdings, types of holdings, and so on—rather than, as we did, in the all one, then the other pattern. We chose the latter because it seemed to us that your entry into the subject of "libraries" would be the library, not the standards; and your question would be, What does my most accessible library offer? rather than, How can I compare the various offerings and then choose a library?

Analogy

If the parts of your subject are not as closely related as, say, types of libraries, you will do better not to force a point-by-point parallelism, but rather to choose the all one, then the other arrangement, making comparisons or contrasts where they exist. When you choose to explain your subject by comparing it to one or more other subjects, your comparison is more accurately termed an analogy: bringing in another related, or analogous, topic because you think it sheds light on yours.

In testing your analogy to see if it will be convincing, ask this question: are you selecting material that is indeed comparable or is the material dissimilar in any ways that may be detected and questioned by your audience? If you can answer yes to the first part of this question and no to the second, you have a valid analogy, one that will strike your audience as logically sound. If your readers don't accept your analogy—if it distracts them from your topic by introducing another which they don't see as related—you may lose them. To keep emphasis where you want it, make sure that your analogy doesn't call attention to itself as dissimilar from your subject in tone. For example, a lot of readers might find silly—or even offensive—an analogy comparing McDonald's restaurants, with their golden arches, to churches, or one comparing McDonald's chief, Ray Kroc, to Chairman Mao (no, we didn't make up either of these). It may help you to avoid problems like this if you imagine your reader to be an expert in the subject of the analogy (religion, Maoist China)—and also a skeptic.

Dialectic

A subset of comparison/contrast development is dialectic. Dialectic is the interplay between an idea (the "thesis"), its opposite ("antithesis"), and the resolution, or "synthesis" of the thesis and antithesis. Consider yourself involved with a dialectic whenever you are dealing with a dynamic process—such as *inventing* a piece of writing. In other words, you are working dialectically whenever you see that opposing ideas—styles, plans, systems, or whatever—can be resolved by a third idea, one that contains parts or aspects of the original opposites. That third idea represents a synthesis—a combining of thesis and antithesis *plus* a creative addition that makes the new thing.

Do any of your subtopics—or your subject as a whole—seem to fill the dialectical pattern of development? The process is really a spiral; that is, often "resolution" can be seen as the first part, or thesis, of a larger problem. A paper that begins by exploring the movement of people to the "sunbelt" might end by asking, in terms of the overall future of America, where should we encourage people to live? Thus, just as thinking dialectically can help you invent your subject outwards to larger subjects of which it is a part or earlier stage, so it can also help you see the relationships among your ideas and your researched material that you are looking for now as you plan the development of your initial ideas into a paper.

A final point. As you develop a comparison/contrast topic—that is, as you outline it—check that each point you cover under the "one" is also covered under the "other" or "others." This is easy to do using the point-by-point arrangement, but requires checking back and forth under the all one, then the other or the dialectical patterns. If we are comparing libraries, we must discuss types of holdings in urban libraries and also in suburban, university, or special libraries.

ORGANIZING PARTS OF THE PAPER

There are several specific rhetorical principles that can help you decide what will be in your paper and where each part will be. These principles are specific because they are likely to help you organize parts of your paper, rather than the paper as a whole. Some of them could help you shape the whole paper—the fundamental organizing principle of some papers, for example, is *definition* or it is *question and answer,* two of the specific rhetorical patterns we will explore below. But it is more likely that you will use definitions periodically, to clarify key words and concepts (a necessity in a convincing paper, and one often forgotten because you, the writer, understand your subject). And it is likely you will use questions and answers now and again as rhetorical devices to involve your readers, to get their attention: "What might Napoleon have done? He had the following options. . . ."

The rhetorical principles are described in the following topics: setting up the problem by statement and question and answer, qualification by example and by summary of research, definition, and explaining your material and organization.

SETTING UP THE PROBLEM BY STATEMENT

Setting up the problem to be explored in your paper may appear to be the same as explaining your material and organization. Certainly, the two rhetorical needs are answered in the same part of your paper —at the beginning. But if your subject, organization, and purpose are relatively simple, you will not need an explanation. On the other hand, you will always have to introduce the problem, or thesis, your paper will explore and do this as clearly as possible.

The two elements in setting up the problem statement are the subject and what is interesting about it. What do we need to know about it, and why? And, if you want to persuade as well as inform, what should we do about it, and why?

For example, look at this opening:

It is perhaps not by mere coincidence that the widespread political invasion of citizens' privacy has occurred in an atmosphere in which commercial inquiries into the private affairs of individuals have become accepted as part of the price people pay for living in a credit-oriented society.[7]

This opening sentence introduces the problem of "widespread political invasion of citizens' privacy," and implies that what we need to know about the problem is, in the writer's opinion, that it stems from a general "atmosphere" in which official "inquiry" into private lives is tolerated. What we should do about this problem is also implied in this first sentence by words like "invasion" and "price."

Here is the admirably simple and clear opening of a college student's research paper:

One of the most sensitive domestic problems facing our federal government is the rising cost of health care. Solutions to this problem are sought by three "special interest" groups, namely, the patients, the physicians, and the politicians.[8]

The first sentence states the problem, and the second introduces both the form and the content of the paper, implying that the author

---

[7]Thomas Whiteside, "A Reporter At Large: Anything Adverse?" *The New Yorker,* April 21, 1975, p. 45.

[8]John Stribling, "Cooperative Medicine: An Alternative Health Care System," research paper, Roosevelt University, December 1977.

will go on to relate the role of each of the three "special interest" groups to the overall problem.

SETTING UP THE PROBLEM
BY QUESTION AND ANSWER

In the next two examples topics are introduced by stimulating the reader's interest in learning the answers to questions. Here is the first paragraph of Pauline Bart's essay, "Why Women See the Future Differently from Men":

> How does a child form its picture of the future—the personal future and the larger, public future of which the personal future is only a part? We do not know much about the stages of development of this imagery, but it is clear that almost from birth society sends different messages to different groups, so that boy babies and girl babies begin very early to see their future as distinctly different.[9]

Note also Bart's general to particular pattern: from the child's development to her specific subject—differences between men and women.

Here is another example of a writer introducing a topic with a question. We have numbered the sentences in order to discuss them below.

> [1]What effect will the new types of communications services, and the vastly increased numbers of existing ones, have upon our society and our culture? [2]Before we attempt to answer that, it is worth remembering that it is never possible to foresee the full impact of a major invention, or even of a minor one. [3]Look, for example, at the effect of the humble typewriter. [4]We males have conveniently forgotten just how few were the occupations—and fewer still the respectable ones—open to women a lifetime ago. [5]Mr. Remington changed all that, and the revolution he wrought was trifling compared with that produced by Henry Ford a little later with his Model T.[10]

---

[9]Chapter 3 in *Learning for Tomorrow: The Role of the Future in Education,* ed. Alvin Toffler (New York: Vintage, 1974), p. 33.

[10]Arthur C. Clarke, "The Social Consequences of Communications Satellites," in *Survival Printout: Total Effect,* ed. Leonard Allison, Leonard Jenkins, Robert Perrault (New York: Vintage, 1973), pp. 112-113.

QUALIFICATION BY EXAMPLE

The passage quoted above illustrates the question-and-answer introduction and also the rhetorical devices of qualification by example. Sentence 2 qualifies, or limits, the scope of the first sentence—that is, it forestalls questions from the skeptical reader about the author's ability to predict effects in the field of communications. The third sentence introduces a specific example of the qualification, making it more memorable, as examples always do.

It is especially hard to remember to qualify. By the time we write, we are sure of our points and believe in them. Backing off and seeing the limits of our subject is hard to do. But it is vital if we are to be convincing. Remember our example of falling away from Christianity as the sole cause of present-day unrest and despair: whenever you find yourself making a cosmic generalization like that, back off and play the skeptic toward yourself.

QUALIFICATION BY SUMMARY OF OTHERS' RESEARCH

A particular kind of qualification common to almost all research writing is summary of the research of others in order to validate your research by showing your command over what has already been found out about the subject. Here are two examples:

Two studies conducted during the early 1950's by Smythe (3) and Head (4) and an analysis of dramatic television programming from 1967 to 1969 by Gerbner (1) revealed an amazing stability in the types of characters who populate these programs as well as a gross underrepresentation of women as major characters. Smythe and Head found that about one-third of all the major characters were female. Gerbner found that females made up roughly one-fourth of all leading characters. Smythe and Gerbner found that female characters were younger than male characters. Gerbner also noted that women—who aged faster than men—were most often cast when family or romantic interests played an integral part in the plot. While only one-third of the male characters were portrayed as married or about to be married, two-thirds of the females were so presented.[11]

[11]Nancy S. Tedesco, "Patterns of Prime Time," *Journal of Communication,* 24:2 (Spring 1974), 119. Note that Tedesco does not employ the standard footnote form we recommended in Chapter 5. Instead, she uses a method commonly employed in science and social science research—referring by number to items in a list of sources at the end of her article.

In this next example, Clara Thompson is introducing her "rebuttal" of Freud. Perhaps because she is refuting a coworker of such great stature, Thompson summarizes Freud's theory in detail, ending with her rejection of his theory and introduction of her own—in the form of a rhetorical question. There are several things to observe here: how to summarize a lengthy and a complex source, Thompson's use of comparison and contrast—girl and boy—in paragraph one, her assumption that her audience has some basic knowledge of psychology—she does not define the key Freudian terms, *Oedipus complex, castration* and *superego*. But the most important is that she clearly identifies her source: "According to Freud . . . ," and, at the beginning of paragraph two, a reminder: "Furthermore, according to Freud . . ." Thompson's third paragraph tells what she has done in its first sentence, then sets up her problem, or "consideration," in the second and third sentences.

According to Freud, because of the little girl's discovery that she has no penis she enters the Oedipus complex with castration already an accomplished fact, while in the little boy the threat of castration arises as a result of the Oedipus complex and brings about its repression. Out of this situation in the little boy Freud believes much that is important in the superego takes its origin. Since the little girl, feeling herself already castrated, need fear no further threat she has less tendency to repress her Oedipus complex and less tendency to develop a superego.

Furthermore, according to Freud, one fact which reinforces the high evaluation of the penis by the little girl is that she is at the time of its discovery unaware that she has a vagina. She therefore considers her clitoris her sole sexual apparatus and is exclusively interested in it throughout childhood. Since she believes this is all she has in place of a penis this emphasizes her inferiority. In addition, the ignorance of the vagina makes for her a special hazard at puberty because the onset of menstruation brings awareness of her female role and requires her to give up her interest in the clitoris and henceforth to seek sexual satisfaction by way of the vagina. With this comes a change in her character. She gives up her boyish aggressiveness and becomes femininely passive.

These are the highlights of the more strictly biologic aspects of Freud's theory of the development of women. I shall touch presently on some other details, but now I wish to review the gross outline in the light of my first consideration, the problem aspect of the biology of woman. The question must be asked: Is this the true story of the biologic sexual development of women?[12]

Summarizing the research of others on your subject, so as to clarify or "stake out" your position, is the beginning; throughout your paper, wherever it is appropriate, you must incorporate the research of others, refuting, correcting, or supporting it, and in each case, identifying it in a footnote so that your readers can check for themselves. Your research paper thus will contain summaries of what others have written and said about your subject and, where the exact words of those people are essential, some quoted matter. Note that both Tedesco and Thompson identify their sources in their text ("according to so and so"); they do not depend solely on footnotes or references to tell the reader who they are referring to. This aids the integration of the author's ideas and those of his or her sources. In the next chapter, we will go into more detail on the manner of presenting sources for research.

DEFINITION

Next, we will present an example of the very common technique of defining as a way of introducing a topic clearly. In this example, the authors define their subject, "paranoia," in a common pattern:

1. They begin with what they claim is the essential meaning of paranoia," in this case, drawn from psychology ("mental-health professionals"):

> Paranoia is a word on everyone's lips, but only among mental-health professionals has it acquired a tolerably specific meaning.

2. They follow with a specific example:

> It refers to a psychosis based on a delusionary premise of self-referred persecution or grandeur (e.g., "The Knights of Columbus control the world and are out to get me . . .").

3. Then, they give more detailed summary definition:

---

[12]Clara M. Thompson, *On Women* (New York: New American Library, 1971), pp. 126–127.

The traditional psychiatric view is that paranoia is an extreme measure for the defense of the integrity of the personality against annihilating guilt. . . .

(Note that this summary uses words with special meanings within a field, in this case, psychology. If you use words of this sort—jargon—you must define those your particular audience might not understand).

4. The authors support their definition with the history of the word's meaning; that is, its *etymology:*

Paranoia is a recent cultural disorder. It follows the adoption of rationalism as the quasi-official religion of Western man and the collapse of certain communitarian bonds (the extended family, belief in God . . .) which once made sense of the universe in all its parts. . . .

Strictly speaking, there was no such thing as paranoia before the mid-nineteenth century, when the word (from the Greek for "beside" and "mind") first surfaced as one of several medical-sounding euphemisms for madness. In an earlier age, the states of mind now explained as paranoia were accounted for differently. . . .

5. They make the transition to their main consideration, present-day paranoia, by using etymology again, and also specific examples:

Even more recent is the wholesale adoption of the terms "paranoia" and "paranoid" into everyday speech. . . . In this context the meanings of the term are blurry but readily comprehensible. "Man, are you ever paranoid." This is not meant as a compliment. . . . "No, thanks, man, I get really paranoid when I smoke dope." Here paranoia is merely a euphemism for fear. . . .

6. And, finally, they conclude their introduction with the specialized definition of paranoia they are most interested in:

In politics, paranoia is a logical consequence of the wrenching loose of power from the rigid social arrangements that once conditioned its exercise, and the resulting preoccupation with questions of "dominate or be dominated." Political and quasi-political notions, such as the conviction that the telephone company is manipulating reality in order to control one's mind, appear routinely in the delusions of persons

suffering from paranoid psychosis. In American public life
Hofstadter showed in *The Paranoid Style in American Po*
cutory themes have cropped up periodically from the beginning. . . .

(Note how smoothly the source is worked into Hertzberg and McClelland's test: ". . . as Richard Hofstadter showed in . . .")

These are the keys to effective definition: essential, or most
common, definition, developed to the extent your audience and
purpose require; etymology, or broad- and long-term view of the
term's meaning; examples; and smooth transition to your specialized
definition. A few other ways to define, not revealed in this example,
are comparison of your term to terms that are the same (synonyms),
similar (analogues), or opposite (antonyms), and definition by function—for example, how does paranoia function, or operate, in contemporary culture? In papers that are wholly or centrally definitions,
you will want to use these various types of definition as your subtopics, developing most if not all of them.

EXPLAINING YOUR MATERIAL
AND ORGANIZATION

Another rhetorical principle to apply to the development of your
material is explaining the material or its organization. This does not
refer to a simplistic, wooden statement, such as "I am going to write
about . . . First, I will cover . . ." As we said earlier, if your subject,
organization, and purpose are relatively simple, you can rely on
topic introductions and connective transitional words and phrases,
such as "moreover," "on the other hand," "the primary cause . . . ,"
and so on, to reveal your purpose.

But suppose that you are writing up particularly unfamiliar or
complex material, or material you are developing in a way you think
your reader might find unusual (say, inductively, with the generalization coming only at the end, after many pages of particulars). Or,
perhaps you are going to leave out some aspects of the subject you
think your reader may fault you for omitting. (See our example,

---

[13]Hendrik Hertzberg and David C. K. McClelland, "Paranoia," *Harper's Magazine*,
June 1974, pp. 51–52.

following.) In these cases, and any others that make you, the writer, feel an introductory explanation is necessary, write one—as clearly as you can. Outlining your paper, discussed at the end of this chapter, can help you; in addition, here is an example of an introductory explanatory statement.

Stanley Rosner and Lawrence E. Abt, editors of a collection of interviews on *The Creative Experience,* begin their preface with a short paragraph proclaiming "there is an ever-widening interest . . . about the creative process . . . , and accordingly, there is an ever-increasing amount of research . . . on . . . the subject." After this introductory "come-on," their second and third paragraphs summarize this research, and in paragraph four, they place themselves within the subject.

> As psychologists, the editors of this volume are naturally most inclined toward inquiry regarding the psychological factors involved in creative development, and this book is an expression of that interest. However, our orientation is substantially sociological as well, because we believe the individual can be studied and understood best within the context of his environment, considered in the widest sense.

Rosner and Abt then go on to describe their methodology—how they picked the creators they interviewed, the questions they asked, and other conditions of the interviews. From this section of their preface, the paragraph introducing the summary description of their interviews is worth noting as an example of an explanation designed to forestall possible complaints from some readers:

> In no sense can we regard our inquiry as scientific, if, by scientific, one means an impeccable methodology that meets all or most of the requirements of experimental procedure. Our inquiry has no such pretensions; its principal aim has been a serious interest in a preliminary understanding of creativity *as experience,* which we regard as largely subjective, though nonetheless capable of communication and understanding.[14]

Of course, these examples are from a book; an introduction to a short paper would be much shorter—never more than a fraction of the total length of the paper.

---

[14](New York: Delta, 1972), pp. vii-viii. Originally published, New York: Grossman, 1970.

REVIEW: ORGANIZATIONAL CHARTS

The following is a summary of all the possible arrangements of material discussed in this chapter, in the form of a chart of each major pattern. Reviewing these patterns should help you make preliminary decisions about your pattern of organization. Which arrangements fit your purpose? Which do not? Make notes on arrangements which you think may help you, and why. Your decisions should be preliminary until you test them against your collection of note cards—the *content* of your paper.

A cautionary word: charts are not hard and fast rules, but rather guidelines to help you plot clear, convincing papers. As models, they should not restrict needed variations. And, again, remember that they may apply both to your whole paper and to parts of it.

In. all cases, the letter A represents your principal subject. As used in these charts, the word *contains* means that the elements listed as contained are included in the larger element (B is contained in A, for example). But the larger element may contain other things as well (A may contain more than B). *Consists of* means that the larger element does not contain any smaller elements other than those listed (A consists of B through G *only*).

1. General to Particular/Particular to General

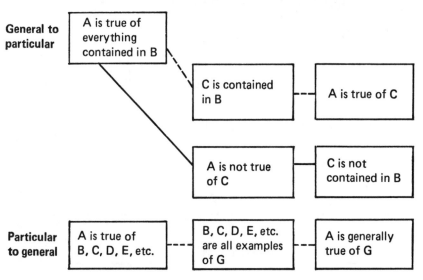

General to particular is the most basic form of argument; it can work in two ways. By following the dotted top line in the general-to-particular chart, you arrive at a logical syllogism: If mortality (A) is true of all human beings (B), and John Doe (C) is a human being (that is, is "contained in" B), then it follows that Doe is mortal. By following the unbroken line in the lower part of this chart, you arrive at one of the most common methods of critical evaluation. For example, A is true of all good plans; A is not true of plan C; therefore, C is not a good plan. The particular-to-general chart, on the other hand, represents a thought process akin to the scientific method. For example, A is true of all these chemicals; all these chemicals (B–E) are of this particular kind (G); therefore we may hypothesize that A is generally true of chemicals of this kind (substitute a characteristic for A—say, sleep inducement—and see how this inductive or scientific process works).

2. Analysis

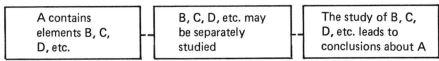

A contains elements B, C, D, etc.	B, C, D, etc. may be separately studied	The study of B, C, D, etc. leads to conclusions about A

Written analysis presents your breakdown of a subject into its parts and your examination of those parts with the purpose of concluding something about the whole subject (A).

3. Chronology

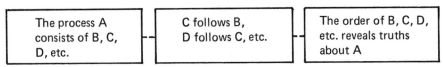

The process A consists of B, C, D, etc.	C follows B, D follows C, etc.	The order of B, C, D, etc. reveals truths about A

Chronology is a form of analysis applied to a process, or series of events, which is broken down into parts, and the parts then analyzed in the order in which they occur in the process.

4. Spatial

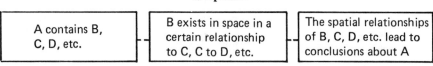

A contains B, C, D, etc.	B exists in space in a certain relationship to C, C to D, etc.	The spatial relationships of B, C, D, etc. lead to conclusions about A

This is another form of analysis, in which component parts of the subject are examined in terms of their relationships in space—it is a useful way of dealing with problems of population distribution, urban problems, and the like.

5. Least to Most

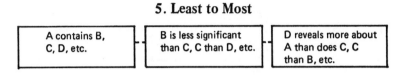

| A contains B, C, D, etc. | B is less significant than C, C than D, etc. | D reveals more about A than does C, C than B, etc. |

This kind of development imparts information dramatically. The process may be reversed, of course, working from most significant to least—but then, to avoid an anticlimatic ending, conclude with a *restatement* of the more significant material.

6. Simple to Complex

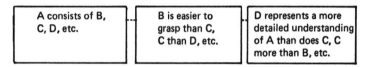

| A consists of B, C, D, etc. | B is easier to grasp than C, C than D, etc. | D represents a more detailed understanding of A than does C, C more than B, etc. |

If your subject may be difficult for the reader to understand, this method—explaining the simpler things first—can be very helpful.

7. Cause/Effect

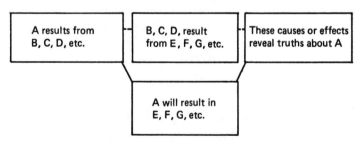

| A results from B, C, D, etc. | B, C, D, result from E, F, G, etc. | These causes or effects reveal truths about A |

A will result in E, F, G, etc.

Two possible methods are involved here. In the first (the dotted top line of the chart), you trace the causes of your subject back as far as you think necessary in order to reveal significant truths—no matter how "removed" these causes are. In the second (the unbroken lower line), you project future effects based on past examples. In these patterns, remember to distinguish between necessary, contributory, and sufficient causes.

8. Comparison/Contrast

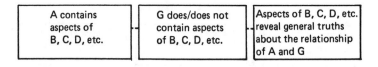

This is a convenient method when you are dealing with two equally important subjects, or with a subject you think can be clarified by comparison, or analogy, to another subject more familiar or attractive to your audience. You can arrive at general conclusions about the subjects by discovering what aspects they do or do not have in common. The important thing to test is the *parallelism* between the items you are comparing.

9. Dialectic

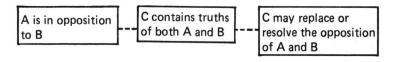

A type of comparison/contrast, this can be an effective method if your subject involves ideas that are in opposition to one another, but can be resolved when seen as parts of a larger whole.

10. Definition

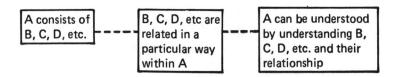

Closely related to analysis, the method of definition emphasizes explaining a concept fully and precisely. It is useful in developing novel, unfamiliar, or controversial subjects, or new terms or words used in a specialized way.

11. Qualification

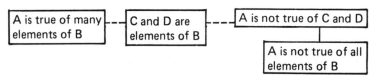

Qualification can help you limit and more precisely define your subject, and in argument help disprove an accepted generalization or stereotype by emphasizing exceptions to the accepted "rule," thus suggesting further exceptions and perhaps a new rule.

Now test these patterns against your subject as a whole, and against its parts, as you arrange your note cards into the outline of your paper.

THE PROCESS OF OUTLINING

Although we have described patterns of organizing material and preparing an outline from note cards in separate sections, in reality you will be working concurrently at the two basic "prewriting" jobs: (1) arranging your note cards, and (2) finding the order that most clearly expresses your subject and most convincingly conveys your purpose to your audience.

PRELIMINARY STEPS

Topics and Subtopics

Your first step is to arrange your note cards according to topics and subtopics. To do this, give each card a *heading* in the upper right corner (for example, Popular Artists: John Travolta: Schooling). To help integrate your ideas into those of others, you may want, as you arrange your cards, to insert those cards noting your ideas among those noting your researched material. As you begin to arrange your notes, you may discover that you have put too much information on a card; if you think you can use that information in two or three different places in your paper divide it and write it up on as many different cards as you see potential topics. In the long run, this is worth the time and the note cards.

Patterns of Development

The next step is to consider potentially persuasive rhetorical arrangements for your topic and subtopics. The problem is that the more knowledge and creativity you bring to arranging your cards, the more connections you will see, and thus the more topics. Before you start even a preliminary outline, much less a draft of your paper, you will probably arrange and rearrange your note cards many times—always testing your arrangements against the rhetorical principles discussed in the first part of this chapter. Is this a place for *definition*? Should a *cause-effect* chain be explained *chronologically*? Should this particular research material be *summarized*, or should it be presented in detail?

When you begin your outline, your topics and subtopics should be arranged in the most convincing order you can work out, selecting the rhetorical principles and forms that suit your material, your purpose, and your audience. As you arrange note cards, you will frequently see the possibility of more than one pattern of development. At these crossroads explore all the possibilities before choosing; this exploration may give you the clues you are looking for on focus, or emphasis, in your paper.

For example, suppose you are doing a paper on Harry Truman's presidency, and you wonder if the subtopic "Truman's dropping the atomic bomb on Japan" belongs under the topic "Truman's foreign policy," "Truman the politician," or "Truman the person." Your research has revealed that Truman's decision to drop the atomic bomb on Japan in 1945 could fit under any of those three topics: it falls into the class of foreign policy decisions; it was affected by political concerns; and there is evidence that it was, personally, a momentous choice. The fact that this decision touches on so many Truman topics is what is potentially creative. If this subtopic—this example of a Truman problem and decision—indicates so much about Harry Truman's presidency, perhaps it should be a focus in your paper. Perhaps it should even be *the* focus. Be alert to emphases that announce themselves, as by overlapping of topics.

Much of the success of your paper depends on emphasis; that is, on how you arrange your material. It might even be argued that when you outline you have the greatest freedom to be creative. Artistry is involved now, for you can no more present an assemblage of facts and ideas loosely strung together than you can present a bowlful of eggs, milk, flour, and sugar and call it a cake. And if you fail to combine all your elements successfully, the result is a mess— just as if you were to combine your cake ingredients in random order. What you need (if we may carry this analogy to cooking just one step further) is a recipe—that is, an outline.

What an Outline Reveals

The process of outlining may reveal gaps in research, unsupported generalizations or assumptions your readers may question. It may also show you where the "seams" are likely to be in your final paper—where you need to test logical connections between the parts of your research, where you need to work out smooth transitions from one point to another.

The outline is such a poor stepchild—after all, we think, usually it doesn't have to be turned in with the final paper, so what do the "rules" of outlining matter? *But the rules reflect the outline's purpose*—the form embodies the function—and so, unless serendipity steps in, a poorly conceived outline will usually evolve into a chaotic paper. Just as the girders in a building may not show, the outline may not be immediately evident in a final paper (and indeed, if the outline is too evident, the paper may come through as too mechanistic), but if the outline is missing, the structure of the paper will probably fall down.

PARALLELISM AND SUBORDINATION IN OUTLINING

Perhaps the most important general rule for productive outlining is derived from the principle of parallelism, that is, your major points should be parallel, or of equal importance to each other. If you are doing a paper on the impact of Darwin's theory of evolution on modern thought, you may well come across some facts about Darwin's childhood, and you may make note of these, thinking they may later prove useful. If you later decide to focus on the development of Darwin's imaginative powers, such notes will of course be crucial: "Darwin's Childhood" could be a major heading in your paper. But if your major topic remains the impact of evolutionary theory on our lives, your focus would blur if you made "Childhood" a division equal, say, to "The impact of Darwin's theory on religion."

In this case you would have to decide whether to use your material on Darwin's childhood at all. But if you decide to use the material, then you need to decide with which *other* topics it is parallel and to which it should be subordinated. In other words, make sure that none of the headings in your outline really belongs under another, larger heading. "Fundamentalist reactions to Darwin" should not be a parallel heading to "The impact of Darwin's theory on religion," since the latter heading includes the former, a type, or subset, of religion called "fundamentalist."

Look at the following short examples in order to practice parallel and subordinate outlining. What is wrong with these outlines?

Maya Angelou	*Day-Care Centers*
I. Childhood	I. Types
II. Autobiographies	II. Philosophies
III. Poetry	III. Those that use "mothers' helpers"
	IV. Volunteerism

In the Maya Angelou example, the outline confuses focus on the woman herself (for example, the period of her childhood) with research into her writing (her autobiographies and her poetry). Items II and III are parallel, but I belongs to a different paper, unless you revise it to "childhood writing" because your research tells you that her childhood writing influenced her adult writing (II and III).

In the Day-Care Centers paper, I (Types) and II (Philosophies) are parallel, but III relates to a type of day-care center and thus should be a subcategory under I; similarly, IV—Volunteerism—is a type of philosophy, and thus should be subsumed under II.

Another note of caution: If you think of an outline as just "busy-work," you can be tempted to put down something like this:

I. Introduction

II. Darwin's theory of evolution

III. Conclusion

In reality this is not an outline, since it does not indicate a series of subtopics or their organization. "Introductions" and "Conclusions" are necessary parts of anything one writes, not divisions of particular subjects; thus, "Introduction" and "Conclusion" alone give you, the writer, no help in developing a structure for your paper that fulfills your purpose.

SUBDIVIDING

Once you have decided what the major divisions of your paper are, you will begin to create the outline in greater detail by subdividing the main topics into smaller ones. Remember that subdividing means there are at least two parts: You cannot break a stick without having at least two smaller sticks, and you cannot break a topic down without having at least two smaller parts. When you look at the main topics of your outline, ask the same questions as when you divided the overall subject: what are its major parts and how are they parallel? If a topic cannot be divided into at least an A *and* a B under each major part (I and so on), then subheadings are not appropriate. Logic tells us that if there is only one subheading under a heading, that subheading must have the same content as the heading, and thus should not be listed separately. So, in the following example, the division of I is wrong and II is logical.

   I.   A.

  II.   A.
         B.

OUTLINE FORM

In order to make your headings and subheadings easy to follow, use the accepted form of indenting each successive subhead, and use the following numbers and letters to indicate increasingly smaller divisions:

   I.
     A.
       1.
         a.
           i. (lower-case Roman numeral)
           (a)

You can see how outlining works by looking at the division of the chapters in this book. Parallel and subordinate topics are indicated typographically rather than by numbers.

SENTENCE OR TOPIC OUTLINES

Your outline may be a sentence outline, with each heading and subheading a full sentence, or it may be a topic outline, with only phrases or words indicating the topic covered. It may be more helpful to use a full-sentence outline, since it will force you to consider what you actually have to say at each point in the paper and help you avoid the temptation of inventing easy subheadings just because (for example) you happen to have one or two cards on that topic. Furthermore, full sentences make the outline easier to work from when you are writing the paper. If, while writing, you notice that your next topic to be covered is "atomic bomb," you may have forgotten exactly what your point was about the bomb. A full sentence in the outline, such as "The fifties' chief 'bogeyman' was the atomic bomb," avoids this problem. Finally, choose one or the other type of outline. If some headings are sentences, others are partial sentences, and still others are just words or phrases, you are likely to have more trouble writing a coherent and well-balanced paper. Watch also that the headings are syntactically parallel, as, Autobiography, Poetry, Drama; or, Childhood Writing, Adult Writing, Writing in Old Age. If you carry that parallelism over to the paper, it will help you relate your topics clearly.

TOPIC SENTENCE

When you think you have completed the outline, test it to see if, in fact, it does express in skeleton form the pattern of your paper. Do this by writing a topic sentence for the whole paper—a statement that summarizes the information and judgments about, and the attitude toward, the subject you hope to convey. Then check the outline to make sure that it develops and supports your topic sentence. Look for contradictions between the topic sentence and headings. Look for "maverick" headings, covering material that isn't "tucked up" under your topic sentence. Hardest of all, look for what *isn't* in the outline; that is, for material needed to support what you say in your topic sentence but which you never researched, wrongly discarded from your pile of usable note cards, or perhaps put in your outline but mistakenly subordinated. On the other hand, your draft of a topic sentence may be too broad, too narrow, or just "off," in relation to the topics you have outlined. Go back and forth between the sentence and the headings in the outline, adding and correcting until you have a "fit" that fulfills your purpose. For examples, see the topic sentences that accompany the sample outlines on pages 115–116.

Like the invention process, to which it is so similar, outlining your paper requires much thoughtful work. But, as with invention, take comfort from the fact that if an outline is well developed, it makes writing your first draft easier by helping you avoid those periods of wondering what to write next and the angry frustration of realizing you have left out a major part of your argument. Writers who respect the outline—that is, experienced, practicing writers—generally say that after it is done, the paper seems to "write itself."

The following two sample outlines illustrate basic patterns of organization: One is a topic outline for a paper on management by objectives, which illustrates the general-to-particular method of organization: the author first plans to establish the general principle that management by objectives is a useful administrative concept, then shows that it can be applied to the specific situation of college administration. The second is a sentence outline that illustrates the principle of analysis, or moving from specifics to a general conclusion. The author first will examine specific elements of the "ancient astronauts" theory, then will attempt to draw a general conclusion about the validity of the theory.

Management by Objectives in Higher Education

Topic sentence: Management by objectives is a managerial technique that may be used in a college.

    I. Management by objectives

        A. What it is
        B. How it was developed
        C. Why businesses should use it

   II. The college as a business
        A. Similarity of structure
            1. Administrative
            2. Financial
        B. Similarity of social function

  III. Management by objectives: in the college
        A. Advantages
        B. Potential problems

Ancient Astronauts?

Topic sentence: Many aspects of the "ancient astronauts" theory may be accounted for by other means.

    I. Much evidence seems to support the theory.
        A. The Nazca Plain drawings suggest prehistoric aircraft.
        B. Aztec tomb drawings apparently depict space travel.
        C. Easter Island statues are evidence of advanced engineering science.

   II. But historical and anthropological research also explains these mysteries.
        A. The Nazca Plain drawings are religious and astronomical figures.
        B. Aztec tomb drawings employ traditional Aztec symbolism.
        C. Easter Island statues can be made without advanced technology.

  III. Is the theory valid on the basis of these examples?
        A. Specific evidence can be explained without the theory.
        B. Logical inference from evidence does not require such an elaborate theory.

5

Research Form

This chapter is a "how to" text, or a "dictionary" that will help you form your research paper based on the principle of incorporating your research with your own ideas. It has three sections: incorporating research into your text by quoting and paraphrasing; citing sources through footnotes and bibliography; and rewriting and proofreading your paper.

TURNING YOUR NOTES INTO TEXT: PROBLEMS IN RESEARCH WRITING

We'll begin with the problem of distinguishing among your research what you should quote and what should be paraphrased, or translated into your own words, and how to paraphrase your sources clearly and fairly.

WHAT TO QUOTE; WHAT TO PARAPHRASE

In *Zen and The Art of Motorcycle Maintenance,* Robert Pirsig used the term *gumption,* as a synonym for *creativity:* "A person filled with gumption doesn't sit around dissipating and stewing about things. He's at the front of the train of his own awareness, watching to see what's up the track and meeting it when it comes. That's gumption." We would want to quote Pirsig rather than paraphrase him because his use of "gumption" for "creativity" is unusual enough that no other work—no synonym of ours—would do. On the other hand, in a paper on evolutionary theory we would state that Charles Darwin paid special note to data unfavorable to his hypotheses because he knew that he would forget this kind of data more easily than he would forget the evidence he wanted to find. In this instance we paraphrase because fact, not judgment or feeling, is being reported, and none of the original words used to report it are unusual.

In general, you should quote when you feel that your source's words express the meaning as no other words could, or express it in an especially striking and memorable way—even if the word or words are not themselves unusual. Particularly, you should quote if your source is describing complicated or unfamiliar processes or states. Also, quote if you are reporting opposing viewpoints; then you can be sure you are fairly reporting all sides of the argument. Whenever a source seems to use a word or words in an unusual or particular way, you'll be on the safe side if you quote. (In these cases, the sources will usually call attention to themselves by saying something like, "I am using the word 'image' in a special way . . .")

HOW TO PARAPHRASE CLEARLY AND FAIRLY

But don't overquote! If you do, *you* will disappear from your paper. Summarizing your source's ideas is one of the best ways to understand them, and putting these ideas into your own words is the key to making them your own.

In paraphrasing, there are several rules to follow. First, do not change important fact-based words (the source's judgment or feeling words would, of course, be quoted, as we indicated above). Second, choose synonyms, or substitute words, that convey the same meaning— even the nuances or shades of meaning—of your source's words. Note how we can paraphrase W. I. B. Beveridge, in *The Art of Scientific Investigation,* on Darwin:

> *Beveridge:* "When Darwin came across data unfavorable to his hypothesis, he made a special note of them because he knew they had a way of slipping out of the memory more readily than the welcome facts."

> *Paraphrase:* ". . . whenever he uncovered data unfavorable to his hypothesis, he noted them especially, because he knew he was more likely to forget them than he was the supporting data."

Suppose we had substituted *theory* or the even vaguer word *idea,* for *hypothesis*—we would have lost the scientific connotation, or nuance, of "hypothesis." If we had said, "he knew he would forget . . . ," instead of, "he knew he was more likely to forget," we would have implied that forgetting was more likely to happen than Beveridge suggested in his phrase, "they had a way of slipping out of the memory." You must be sure of your source's meanings before you can paraphrase instead of quoting. Finally, don't forget that you need to footnote a paraphrase just as you do a quotation. The page or pages you give in your note should cover the entire range of source material you have paraphrased.

WHAT TO FOOTNOTE

Footnote (1) all direct quotations or exact words of a source; (2) any idea not your own; (3) facts that are not generally known; and (4) lengthy factual matter which you are summarizing.

Lengthy Matter

It is particularly easy to forget to footnote the lengthy, largely factual matter that seems to you basic, uncontroversial "background" to your subject; for example, a description of how atomic reactors work in a paper focused on their controversial locations. But as uncontroversial as your background material may appear to you, a footnote adds to your credibility—and also serves the reader who, if your paper is interesting, may want to read more on the subject.

For a summary paragraph or two on background history, description or definition, you can use a single, summary footnote at the end, giving all your sources and, if it would be helpful, noting which aspects of the material each source covers. If you cite more than one source in a footnote, separate the notes on each source by semicolons.

Little-Known Facts

An example of documenting a little-known fact might be a footnote to W. I. B. Beveridge on Darwin's habit of making special note of data unfavorable to his hypotheses. On the other hand, one wouldn't footnote Darwin's birth and death dates, because such information is widely available in encyclopedias, almanacs, and the like. But if you are in doubt about how little or how well known a fact is—footnote your source.

Exact Words and Ideas

In this text we have quoted words that a number of people have used to express ideas. Others were paraphrased. Both quotations and paraphrases were footnoted. At the same time, we have tried to show that few, if any, ideas "belong" solely to anyone. Researchers fairly new to their fields have to be careful not to assume that their source's version of an idea is the complete idea or the original source. You won't fall into this error if you research widely enough, and particularly if you follow the clues in your sources as to others who contributed to the idea. For example, in Chapter 4 Clara Thompson refers to Freud's theory of female identity and Nancy Tedesco to other social scientists who have explored the image of women in prime-time television. Needless to say, you can't trace every idea to all its sources and variants, but do follow up what seem to be your source's sources that are most relevant to your subject.

Try always to cite the original source. Don't, for example, quote Thompson's quotation from Freud; go to Freud. Your secondhand source may be quoting erroneously or out of context. If, because you cannot find the original, you must quote or paraphrase from a secondary source, in your footnote give as much bibliographical information on the original as you can find.

INCORPORATING RESEARCH INTO YOUR TEXT

Cohesiveness and Respect for Sources

The main criterion of good writing is cohesiveness, that is, we try to make the parts of papers, memos, letters, hold together, relate clearly to each other and to our overall purpose. In research papers, cohesiveness depends on how smoothly, how "seamlessly," we weave our research—the ideas and words of others—into our own text. In addition to being cohesive, we want to be convincing; thus we need to show that we are being fair to our sources. For this reason, research must not only be incorporated smoothly, it must be clearly distinguished from *our* ideas.

Both aims—cohesiveness and respect for sources—are illustrated by the last paragraph on tail fins quoted in Chapter 4:

By 1960, however, economic considerations altered the purchasing habits of the nation. Compacts had been introduced and styling in general became more austere. In 1959, Ford staff stylist Elwood P. Engel said, "Price is the most important thing on the small car, economy of operation is second and then styling, I would say. The owner is buying transportation and economy, not styling."

The paragraph begins with the authors' generalizations, supported by the closing quotation. Note that the source is identified in the text, in addition to a footnote (we have omitted the footnote here). As we said in Chapter 4, textual identification of sources is an important aid to readers' understanding, and one that beginning research writers frequently omit if they give a footnote to the source.

Note the confusion when a writer neglects either to claim an idea or attribute it to a source. The following is from a student's paper:

> The most satisfying approach to reading poetry is one which enables the reader to sense the music, mood, and meaning of what the author has written. John Dolman has arranged these three terms in this particular order for a specific reason. In the study of any art it is the form which first captures our attention, for the skill of the artist is conveyed in the strength of his form. . . .

As we read, we aren't sure if the judgment in the last sentence quoted is that of the writer or if it is John Dolman's opinion. Also note that the writer confusingly does not put quotation marks around "music, mood, and meaning," although the next sentence indicates not only that these were Dolman's words, but they had "specific" meaning for him.

Incorporating the Long Quotation

As you can see from the examples throughout this book, the form for incorporating the long quotation is as follows: indent and single-space each and omit the opening and closing quotation marks used with shorter quotations (such as "music, mood, and meaning" above).

How long is a long quotation? Material that would run four or more lines in your paper should be indented (on the typewriter, four spaces from the left margin). If your quotation is the beginning of a paragraph, indent four more spaces. Double space between quoted paragraphs. Although you omit the opening and closing quotation marks in an indented quotation, retain the internal quotation marks of a "quotation within a quotation." Here is an example from Chapter 4:

> . . . In a 1959 survey commissioned by the Fund for the Republic, Patrick McGrady, Jr. wrote: "Television criticism is, by and large, the fitful labor of tired writers of monumental good will, a degree of talent and jaded perspective . . . ."

Poetry Quotations

Poetry quotations should also be indented. Center the quotation on the page, single space, and do not enclose the material in quotation marks. If a line is too long, run it over and indent two spaces as follows:

> A child said *What is the grass?* fetching it
> to me with full hands.

(This is from "Song of Myself," by the nineteenth-century American poet Walt Whitman.)

If you quote nonconsecutive lines from a poem, indicate the omitted line or lines by a full row of double-spaced period marks and double space above and below the row of "dots":

> But at my back I always hear
> Time's wingèd chariot hurrying near:
>
> . . . .
>
> The grave's a fine and private place,
> But, none, I think, do there embrace.

(These lines are from "To His Coy Mistress," by Andrew Marvell, a seventeenth-century English poet.)

Additions and Deletions

Because we quote only to make *our* points, we often want to omit some of our source's words, or to add some of our own. To show omissions, use the *ellipsis;* to show additions, use *brackets.* But remember the reader: too many brackets and ellipses can make a quotation hard to read, and what is more important, they may lead you, the writer, to alter your source's meaning. Generally, either quote in full or summarize in your own words, grammatically incorporating your source's "inescapable" words, and, of course, enclosing them in quotation marks.

Ellipsis for omissions. If you want to omit some words in a quotation, use the ellipsis: three dots (periods) with one space between each dot:

quoted words . . . quoted words

If your quoted words form two or more complete sentences, use four dots to indicate omitted material between them:

quoted words . . . . quoted words . . . .

For example:

"It is over . . . . But it is not forgotten . . . . "

However, if the *source's* sentence ends before the ellipsis, place a period immediately after the last word, followed by three spaced dots:

quoted sentence. . . .

When you omit words, be careful not to change your source's meaning. For example:

Source: Mounting inflation during the 1920s is sometimes too simply regarded as the cause of the Depression.

Researcher's misleading quotation: According to John Doe, "mounting inflation during the 1920s is . . . the cause of the Depression."

By omitting the qualifying words "sometimes too simply regarded as," the researcher has not only changed the source's meaning; he has, in fact, turned it around to an opposite meaning.

Brackets for changes and additions. Brackets are the answer if you need to change a word ending or other part of a word for grammatical reasons, or if you want to add to a quotation.

1. *Brackets for grammatical change:* Example:

Source: I believe television, like radio, is not an art form.

Researcher: John Doe believes that television and radio are not "art form[s]."

2. *Brackets for addition: clarification:* Example: educator Janet Emig describing what she calls "Mozartian" and the "Beethovian" creative types, writes "The creative self in a Beethovian is not a plummeting diver." Quoting this by itself would not make it clear what the creator dives into, because it does not include her earlier words on the Mozartian diving into the unconscious. Thus, we need to add a clarifying phrase in brackets: "The creative self in a Beethovian is not a plummeting diver [into the unconscious], but a plodding miner. . . ."

3. *Brackets for addition: emphasis:* Another reason for using a bracketed insertion is to supply your own emphasis to the material you quote. For example:

Researcher: According to Picasso, art is not just inspiration, but rather, is the "result of *rejected* discoveries." [Italics ours.]

But be sparing with bracketed comments. It is better to make your points in *your* text, rather than interrupting your sources.

Closing Punctuation for Quotations

1. Periods and commas go inside the closing quotation mark—even when the marks enclose only one letter or figure: "A."

2. Semicolons, colons, and dashes go outside the closing quotation mark. For example:

According to John Doe, Marlon Brando is "over-the-hill";[1]
I disagree.

Note that the footnote *follows* all punctuation (except the dash), even when it does not come at the end of a sentence.

3. Exclamation points and questions marks go outside or inside the closing quotation mark, depending upon whether the exclamation point or question mark is part of the material quoted. For example:

Can we agree with John Doe's analysis of Brando as "over-the-hill"?

If the question mark were put inside the quotation mark—Can we agree with John Doe's analysis of Brando as "over-the-hill?"—it would indicate that the question came from the source, not from you.

Summary Example of Using Sources

Here is an example of the progress of an idea from its original source to the note card (which illustrates both quoting and paraphrasing), to a rough draft of a paper, and finally to the completed paper.

The source. From "The Structural Study of Myth," by Claude Levi-Strauss, in *Structural Anthropology,* by Claude Levi-Strauss, translated by Claire Jacobson and Brooke Grundfest Schoepf (New York: Basic Books, 1963), Chapter XI, p. 206.

> Despite some recent attempts to renew them, it seems that during the past twenty years anthropology has increasingly turned from studies in the field of religion. At the same time, and precisely because the interest of professional anthropologists has withdrawn from primitive religion, all kinds of amateurs who claim to belong to other disciplines have seized this opportunity to move in, thereby turning into their private playground what we had left as a wasteland. The prospects for the scientific study of religion have thus been undermined in two ways.

The note card.

> Levi-Strauss, Claude. "The Structural Study of Myth,"
> *Structural Anthropology.* Trans. Claire Jacobson and
> Brooke Grundfest Schoepf. New York: Basic Books,
> 1963, Ch. XI, p. 206.
>
> In last 20 yrs. anthropology "has increasingly turned
> from studies in the field of religion"; "all kinds of
> amateurs . . . have seized this opportunity to move
> in . . . ." Thus the scientific study of religion has
> been undermined.

The rough draft.

> Although religious studies would seem to be an area
> that would provide a wealth of material for anthro-
> pologists, Claude Levi-Strauss, the great French anth-
> ropologist, says that in the last twenty years anthro-
> pology "has increasingly turned from studies in the field
> of religion"; thus "all kinds of amateurs . . . have seized
> this opportunity to move in . . . ."

The completed paper.

> Although religious studies would seem to provide a
> wealth of material for anthropologists, the great French
> anthropologist Claude Levi-Strauss complained in 1963
> that anthropology had for the preceding twenty years
> turned away from this field. As a result, wrote Levi-
> Strauss, "all kinds of amateurs . . . have seized this
> opportunity to move in . . . ."[1]

Notice how the idea is gradually transformed from the original words of the source into a brief quotation that supports the idea the author of the research paper is trying to develop. Much of the original quotation has been left out of the final draft, but to have included the entire passage would have broken the flow of the author's argument. In taking notes, the author copied only those quotations that seemed most relevant, paraphrasing the rest (but, of course, keeping all of Levi-Strauss's meaning). In the rough draft, both the quoted phrases from the notes are retained, but the result creates a slightly awkward sentence and leaves out the vital information that Levi-Strauss was writing in 1963—which changes the meaning of his reference to "the last twenty years." In the final draft, the author has added the information of the date by paraphrasing the quote (also changing "has" to the more accurate "had"), and has also revised the grammar and style by omitting unnecessary phrases such as "an area that would provide" in the first line, and unnecessary commas such as those around the phrase "the great French anthropologist."

Incorporating Footnotes in the Rough Drafts

As you write your first drafts, you will want to note every quotation or paraphrase you need to footnote in the final paper, but *without losing your train of thought.* You can do this in either of two ways: Keep a separate pad of paper, numbering each note consecutively in your draft and on the pad. Or, incorporate the footnote information into your draft copy immediately after the text material you are footnoting. If the latter, draw a line above and below the footnote, separating it from your text.

MAKING THE MOST OF FOOTNOTES
AND BIBLIOGRAPHY

Footnotes and bibliographies are generally underused by writers. The reason they are required in research papers is not (as you may think) to harass you with their exacting formal demands, but rather to communicate information more specialized than the information in your text.

Annotated Bibliography

A bibliography, for example, must tell the reader who wrote what text and where and when it was published. But it can also be used to give the reader additional, succinct information about that text. For example:

> Brodie, Fawn M. *Thomas Jefferson.* New York: W. W. Norton, 1974. Provocative example of psychohistory.

Content Footnotes

You may include your summary or evaluation of the source in your footnote instead of in the bibliography. For example, in a discussion of creativity our first reference to Arthur Koestler's *The Act of Creation* might want to emphasize what we said in the text about how the unconscious is also, like the conscious mind, important to creativity. Our footnote could read:

> [2] *The Act of Creation* is a synthesizing study of the roles of the conscious and unconscious in science and art. (New York: Dell, 1964). . . .

Another kind of footnote is a textual "aside"—for example, the footnote in Chapter 1 (page 1), giving a reference on the history of the meaning of the word *invention.* This information adds to the topic, but is not directly necessary to your understanding how to invent; including it in the text might distract you from the focus. Thus, the footnote here serves as an additional conduit by which to inform and persuade: a medium that is separate from, but still connected to the text.

Another purpose served by the content footnote is to call the reader's attention to other, related texts. For example:

> [1] Besides *The Act of Creation,* see also Robert E. Mueller, *Inventivity: How Man Creates in Art and Science* (New York: The John Day Co., 1963), pp. 85-92, on the ways in which the unconscious shapes the creations of both artists and scientists.

The essential content of your footnotes must be full information about the text you are citing. This means not only author(s), title, publication information (city of publication, publisher, date of publication), and page references, but also any other information that might influence the reader's judgment as to the reliability of your source—the date of the edition of the text you are using, whether it is a revised edition, or perhaps a source and date of original publication. Examples are the Mausner and the Dewey footnotes below:

[1] Bernard and Judith Mausner, "A Study of the Anti-Scientific Attitude," *Frontiers of Psychological Research: Readings from "Scientific American,"* ed. Stanley Coopersmith (San Francisco: W. H. Freeman, 1966), p. 295. Originally published in *Scientific American,* Feb. 1955.

[2] John Dewey, *The Quest for Certainty: A Study of the Relation of Knowledge and Action,* Gifford Lecture, 1929 (London: George Allen & Unwin, Ltd., 1930), pp. 196, 210. Paperback ed.: New York: G. P. Putnam's Sons Capricorn Books, 1960.

In the Mausner example the date of original publication (eleven years earlier) is especially important because the subject is scientific experiment, which dates so quickly. In the Dewey reference we cited our source—the original publication in 1930—but added the information that the book is now available in a paperback edition.

Information about original publication is generally found on the title and copyright pages of books, or on permissions or acknowledgments pages, or in notes at the bottom of the first page of an article in a magazine or anthology.

CITING YOUR SOURCES:
FOOTNOTE AND BIBLIOGRAPHY FORM

To make a footnote, first place a reference number in the text after the material you are citing, half a line above the line of your text (superscript): for example, [1]. Wherever possible, the footnote number should be put at the end of a sentence rather than in the middle, and the footnote number follows *all* punctuation except the dash.

POSITION OF FOOTNOTE IN TEXT

You may choose to type your footnotes at the bottom of the page that has the corresponding text reference or all together at the end of the paper. For example, put the same number in front of, and half a line above, the footnote. For notes typed at the end of the paper, (sometimes called *endnotes* instead of footnotes), some authorities recommend an alternative format: instead of elevating the numeral, as in the text, place it on the same line as the note and follow it with a period and a space. Footnotes placed at the bottom of each page are harder to make because you have to judge how much space to leave on every page. But they are preferable because their information is more accessible than if your readers have to turn back and forth continually between the pages of your text and the footnote pages following the paper. Check with your instructor as to whether he or she has a preference.

If you place footnotes at the bottom of pages, type a line about 1½ inches long, starting from the left margin, two spaces below the last line of text. Leave a double space below this line for the first footnote.

It takes practice to judge accurately how many notes you will have on a page. After you estimate the number, add up the double spaces before and after the 1½-inch rule, the estimated number of lines in each note, the double spaces between notes, and the 1-inch bottom margin. Then make a pencil mark at the right edge of the page, so that you will stop your text with enough space for your notes.

For both footnotes and endnotes, indent each five spaces, as you would a paragraph in a text. Single space wherever more than one line is needed for a footnote, but double space between footnotes.

Number footnotes consecutively throughout the paper; don't start over with [1] at the beginning of each page of your text.

FOOTNOTE FORM

This is standard footnote form:

Author, *title,* special information (city: publisher, date), pages.

For example:

John Doe, *Mirages,* 2d ed. (New York: Art Press, 1978), p. 11.

If you do not give the book's subtitle in the text, include it (and the title) in your footnote. Unless the title page indicates another mark of punctuation, use a colon to set off a subtitle from a title, as: *Mirages: Studies in Illusion.*

Special Publication Information

Special information includes all the additional data that will help your reader evaluate your source. In the example above, it is "2d ed.," meaning this is the second edition of the book *Mirages.*

Following is a list of the most common special publication information and abbreviations used in footnotes:

ed.: edition: Your source is not the first, but a subsequent edition (2d, 3d, etc.). The title page will give you this information. If no edition number is given, your source is the only edition; you do not note "1st ed."

ed.: editor: Your source has been edited by another. For example: John Doe, *Mirages,* ed. Jane Smith (New York: Art Press, 1978), p. 11.

rev. ed.: Your source is a revised edition of the original text. For example: John Doe, *Mirages,* rev. ed. (New York: Art Press, 1978), p. 11. ("Rev. of" is an abbreviation of "review of.")

rpt. Your source was reprinted on the date you give (this is usually used to distinguish between the date of original publication and the date of publication of a paperback edition). For example: John Doe, *Mirages* (New York: Art Press, 1978, rpt. 1979), p. 11.

series title; Your source is one in a series with a title other than
volume   the title of your source. Give series title (not under-
number: lined), followed by the volume number in the series.
              For example: John Doe, *Mirages,* University Studies in
              Illusion, 33 (New York: Art Press, 1977), pp. 12-13.

trans.:   Your source has been translated from another language.
              For example: John Doe, *Mirages,* trans. Mary Brown
              (New York: Art Press, 1977), pp. 12-13.

The author's name, the title of your source, city of publication,
publisher, date of publication, and the page(s) you used are standard
information and (except for page numbers) are found on the title
and copyright pages. In some articles, such as in newsmagazines, the
author is not indicated, and you will begin your footnote with the
title. (But look at the end of the article to be sure that a byline has
not been given.) If the following data are omitted, indicate this in
parenthesis by an abbreviation: no publisher (n. p.), no publication
date (n. d.), no pagination (n. pag.).

Diagrams of Footnote Form

Figures 8-11 give the general footnote form for (1) books; (2)
periodicals or magazines; (3) parts of larger works, such as essays
in books or books in a series; and (4) government documents. The
model footnote appears in the center of each figure. Trace each
line from the model to its boxed explanatory note. Where the note
indicates insertion of special information, check to see if your
source gives that information. If it does, insert it. If not, go on to
the next item in the model. If you follow this form, you will always
have a standard footnote.

Short Forms

When part of the reference is in the text. If the author is named in
your text, limit the footnote information to title, publication data,
and page numbers. If the title of the work is also given in your text,
begin the footnote with the next item—for example, the name of

Figure 8. General footnote form for books.

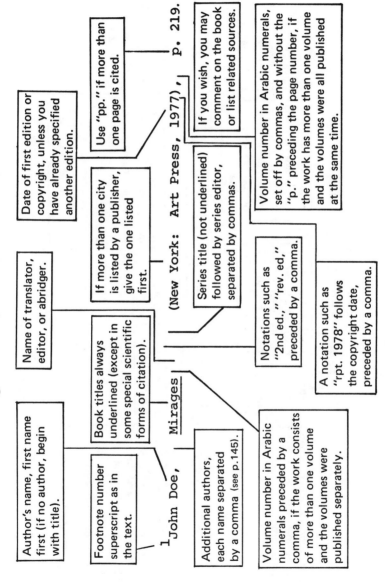

Figure 9. General footnote form for periodicals.

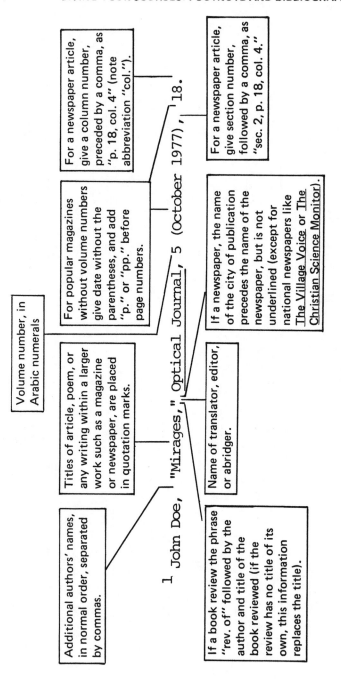

Figure 10. General footnote form for parts of larger works
(essays in books, articles in sources other than periodicals, books in series, etc.).

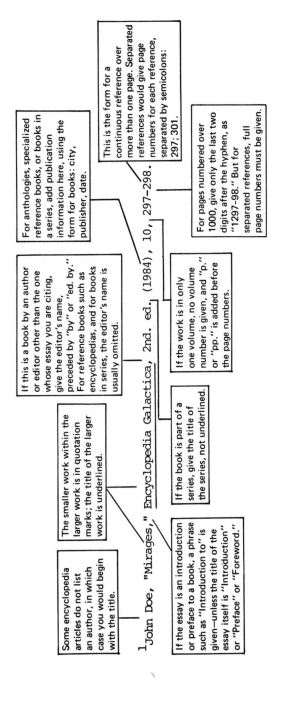

Some encyclopedia articles do not list an author, in which case you would begin with the title.

The smaller work within the larger work is in quotation marks; the title of the larger work is underlined.

If this is a book by an author or editor other than the one whose essay you are citing, give the editor's name, preceded by "by" or "ed. by." For reference books such as encyclopedias, and for books in series, the editor's name is usually omitted.

For anthologies, specialized reference books, or books in a series, add publication information here, using the form for books: city, publisher, date.

This is the form for a continuous reference over more than one page. Separated references would give page numbers for each reference, separated by semicolons: 297; 301.

If the essay is an introduction or preface to a book, a phrase such as "Introduction to" is given—unless the title of the essay itself is "Introduction" or "Preface" or "Foreword."

If the book is part of a series, give the title of the series, not underlined.

If the work is in only one volume, no volume number is given, and "p." or "pp." is added before the page numbers.

For pages numbered over 1000, give only the last two digits after the hyphen, as "1297-98." But for separated references, full page numbers must be given.

[1] John Doe, "Mirages," Encyclopedia Galactica, 2nd. ed., (1984), 10, 297-298.

Figure 11. General footnote form for government documents.
For citing laws, court cases, the Constitution, and the *Congressional Record,* see pp. 144–146.

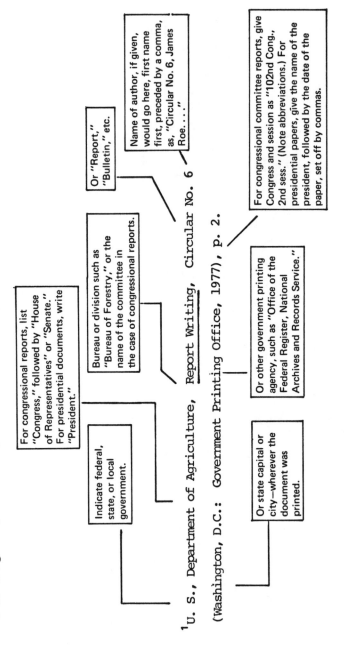

the periodical if you have given the title of the article in your text, or special publication information, or place of publication if you have written a book's title into your text. Thus, if you say in your text, "John Doe states . . . ," your footnote can read

Mirages (New York: Art Press, 1977), pp. 12-13.

If your text says, "In *Mirages,* John Doe states . . . ," the footnote can begin with

(New York: Art Press, 1977), pp. 12-13.

When there is more than one footnote referring to a single source. Subsequent footnotes, after your first reference to work, can also be shortened, and if you use more than one work by the same author, include the title as well as the author to avoid confusion: Doe, *Mirages,* p. 10.

Although it is not generally preferred, you may use Ibid, if the subsequent note follows immediately after the first footnote. If the page(s) referred to are different, use Ibid., pp. 6-10 (for example). Note that Ibid.—Latin for "in the same place"—is not underlined.

Avoid the complicated Latinisms *op. cit.* ("in the work cited") and *loc. cit.* ("in the place cited"). Can *you* figure out the difference between "in the work . . ." and "in the place . . ."? We can't!

The preferred way to refer to the same source in subsequent footnotes is to use a short form of the title (if it will not be confused with other titles): for example, *The Emotional Significance of Imaginary Beings: A Study of the Interaction Between Psychopathology, Literature, and Reality in the Modern World,* by Robert Plank, could, in subsequent footnotes, be cited as Plank, *Emotional Significance.*

When there are repeated references to one text. If you cite from one source heavily, you may indicate at the end of your first footnote to that source that "All subsequent references are to this edition and will be incorporated into the text." Then incorporate these references in parentheses after each citation—paraphrase or quote. For example:

According to John Doe in *Mirages* (p. 23), . . . [paraphrase] or
According to John Doe in *Mirages,* "xxxx" (p. 23). [quotation]

Note that the sentence punctuation *follows* the parenthetical reference.

One footnote for several sources. It is rare that one footnote can serve to identify and differentiate among several sources, but at least one place where this may be appropriate is at the end of your "background" summary. If you have used similar materials from several texts, and if you see no confusion for the reader or unfairness to your different sources, you may list them all in one footnote. Separate each note with a semicolon; and be sure to specifically cite any quotations you have used in your summary. For example:

[1] John Doe, *Mirages* (New York: University Press, 1977), pp. 12–22; James Roe, *Illusions* (Berkeley: Berkeley Press, 1976), pp. 1–8; Jill Lowe, *Desert and Sea* (Bloomington: Bloomington Press, 1975), pp. 34–46; 87–103. The quotation is from Lowe, p. 99.

BIBLIOGRAPHY FORM

Citing your sources in an alphabetical list at the end of your research papers, including those you did not use in your final paper, is a guide for the person who wants to read further in your subject and related subjects.

Comparison of Footnote and Bibliography Form

The bibliography form looks the opposite of footnote form: that is, where footnotes are indented five spaces in their first line, bibliography entries begin at the left margin, and second and subsequent lines are indented five spaces.

Footnote: xxxxxxxxxxxxxxxxxxxxxxxx
xxxxxxxxxxxxxxxxxxxxxxxxxxx

Bibliography: xxxxxxxxxxxxxxxxxxxxxxxxxxx
xxxxxxxxxxxxxxxxxxxxxxx

Because a bibliography is alphabetized, the author's last name appears first:

Bibliography: Doe, John

Footnote: John Doe

Otherwise the same information appears in the same places in the bibliography entry as in the footnote. The differences are in *puncutation,* and these can be summarized as follows: In the bibliography, periods—not commas—appear after the author's name, after the title, and after any special publication information. A comma is used after the publisher and before the date. The parenthesis around publication information is not used in the bibliography (except around the date when the volume of a periodical is given). Page numbers are also generally omitted in the bibliography, except for articles.

The following diagram compares footnote and bibliography form:

Basic Footnote Form

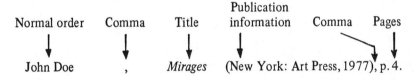

Basic Bibliography Form

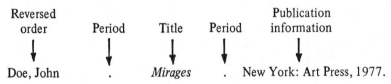

Diagrams of Bibliography Form

Figures 12 and 13 diagram the basic bibliography form for books and periodicals (see pages 145–154 for examples of irregular bibliography and footnote forms). As with the footnote models, follow each line to its explanatory box; then check if that information is available for your source.

Figure 12. General bibliography form for books.

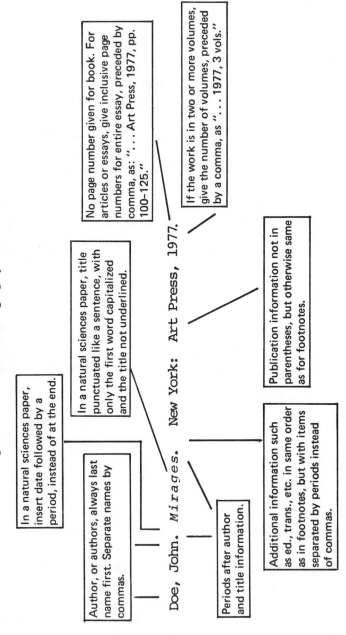

No page number given for book. For articles or essays, give inclusive page numbers for entire essay, preceded by comma, as: ". . . Art Press, 1977, pp. 100–125."

If the work is in two or more volumes, give the number of volumes, preceded by a comma, as ". . . 1977, 3 vols."

In a natural sciences paper, title punctuated like a sentence, with only the first word capitalized and the title not underlined.

In a natural sciences paper, insert date followed by a period, instead of at the end.

Author, or authors, always last name first. Separate names by commas.

Periods after author and title information.

Additional information such as ed., trans., etc. in same order as in footnotes, but with items separated by periods instead of commas.

Publication information not in parentheses, but otherwise same as for footnotes.

Doe, John. *Mirages.* New York: Art Press, 1977.

Figure 13. General bibliography form for periodicals.

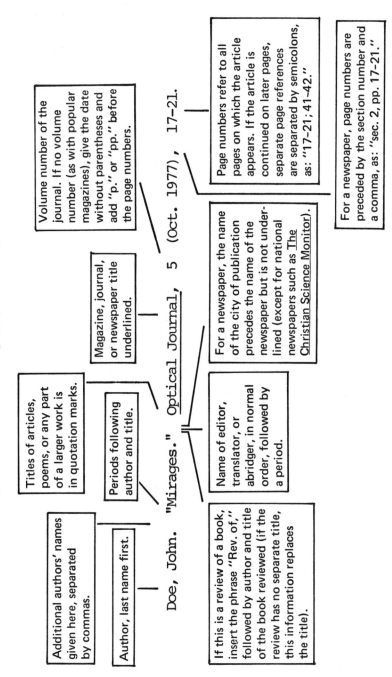

SAMPLE FOOTNOTE
AND BIBLIOGRAPHY ENTRIES

(For samples of irregular footnote and bibliography forms, see pages 145-154.)

Book

Footnote: [1] Midge Mackenzie, *Shoulder to Shoulder* (New York: Alfred A. Knopf, 1975), p. 279.

Bibliography: Mackenzie, Midge. *Shoulder to Shoulder.* New York: Alfred A. Knopf, 1975.

Article in Scholarly Journal

Footnote: [2] Marc Angenot, "Science Fiction in France Before Verne," *Science Fiction Studies,* 5 (March 1978), 59.

Bibliography: Angenot, Marc. "Science Fiction in France Before Verne." *Science Fiction Studies,* 5 (March 1978), 58-67.

Article in Popular Magazine

Footnote: [3] Ponchitta Pierce, "Bill Cosby: Laughter with Lessons," *Readers Digest,* Aug. 1976, p. 111.

Bibliography: Pierce, Ponchitta. "Bill Cosby: Laughter with Lessons." *Readers Digest,* Aug. 1976, pp. 110-115.

Newspaper Article

Footnote: [4] Gerald Eskenazi, "Boston Marathon: Food and Beer," *New York Times,* April 16, 1978, sec. 5, p. 1, col. 2.

Bibliography: Eskenazi, Gerald. "Boston Marathon: Food and Beer." *New York Times,* April 16, 1978, sec. 5, pp. 1, 3.

(Note that "pp. 1, 3" indicates the article begins on p. 1 and is continued on p. 3—a common practice in newspapers.)

Article in Encyclopedia

Footnote: [5] Lawrence I. O'Kelly, "Instinct," *Encyclopedia International,* 1966, 9, 312.

Bibliography: O'Kelly, Lawrence I. "Instinct." *Encyclopedia International,* 1966, 9, 312.

Essay in Book

Footnote: [6] Arthur Knight, "*Citizen Kane* Revisited," *Focus on Citizen Kane,* ed. Ronald Gottesman (Englewood Cliffs, N.J.: Prentice-Hall, 1971), p. 123.

Bibliography: Knight, Arthur. "Citizen Kane Revisited," in *Focus on Citizen Kane,* ed. Ronald Gottesman. Englewood Cliffs, N.J.: Prentice-Hall, 1971, pp. 120–126.

Government Document

Footnote: [7] U.S. Department of Health, Education, and Welfare, *We Want You to Know About Today's FDA,* No. (FDA) 74-1021 (Washington, D.C.: U.S. Government Printing Office, 1975), n. pag.

(Note that "n. pag." indicates that this particular pamphlet does not number its pages.)

Bibliography: U.S. Department of Health, Education, and Welfare. *We Want You to Know About Today's FDA.* No. (FDA) 74–1021. Washington, D.C.: U.S. Government Printing Office, 1975.

Work Consisting of More Than One Volume, Volumes Published Separately

Footnote: [8] Lewis Mumford, *The Pentagon of Power,* vol. 2 of *The Myth of the Machine* (New York: Harcourt Brace Jovanovich, 1970), p. 107.

Bibliography: Mumford, Lewis. *The Pentagon of Power.* Vol. 2 of *The Myth of the Machine.* New York: Harcourt Brace Jovanovich, 1970.

Work Consisting of More Than One Volume, Volumes Published Simultaneously

Footnote: [9] Arthur Schopenhauer, *The World as Will and Idea,* trans. R. B. Haldane and J. Kemp (London: Kegan Paul, Trench, Trübner & Co., 1909), III, 26.

Bibliography: Schopenhauer, Arthur. *The World as Will and Idea.* Trans. R. B. Haldane and J. Kemp. London: Kegan Paul, Trench, Trübner & Co., 1909, 4 vols.

Work With Editor or Abridger

Footnote: [10] Sir James George Frazer, *The New Golden Bough,* ed. Theodor H. Gaster (New York: Criterion, 1959), p. 447.

Bibliography: Frazer, Sir James George. *The New Golden Bough.* Ed. Theodor H. Gaster. New York: Criterion, 1959.

IRREGULAR TYPES IN FOOTNOTES
AND BIBLIOGRAPHY

Examples of the most common irregular forms for footnotes and bibliography entries, and our comments on each, are given below. No comment on a bibliography form indicates that it is regular; that is, it follows standard footnote form for that type, substituting periods for commas.

Additional Authors

For more than three authors, give the first author and then, "et al.," —or the English translation, "and others." Example:

John Doe, et al., *Mirages*. . . .

In *bibliography* entries with two or three authors, reverse only the name of the first author: "Doe, John, James Rowe, Jill Lowe. . . ."

Anonymous Authors

The footnote entry begins with the title.

The Bible and Other Sacred Scriptures

Neither the names of the scriptures nor their books are underlined. The convention is to indicate if you have used other than the King James Version of the Bible. Example:

Matthew 10:34–37 (Revised Standard Version).

In the example, 10 is the chapter number; 34–37 are the verse numbers.

The *bibliography* entry would be simply

The Bible. Revised Standard Version.

Congressional Record

Example:

U.S., Congress, Senate [or House], Senator Smith's tribute to John Doe, 102d Cong., 1st sess., Dec. 10, 1976, *Congressional Record* 4001:6002.

In the example, 4001 is the volume number of the *Congressional Record;* 6002 is the page number. Note the abbreviations of Congress, its number (102d), the abbreviation of "first session," and the abbreviation of the month in the date.

If you use the daily edition of the *Congressional Record,* give the full date (for example, March 24, 1977), because the page numbers in the daily editions and the bound volumes are not the same.

Bibliography form retains the page numbers.

Constitutions

Examples:

U.S., *Constitution,* Art. 2, sec. 2.

Illinois, *Constitution,* Amend. 2, sec. 2.

The abbreviations are Art.: Article; sec.: section; and Amend.: Amendment. If your reference is to a Constitution that was later revised, give the original date in parenthesis after the word *Constitution:*

Illinois, Constitution (1968), Amend. 2, sec. 2.

In the *bibliography,* periods are used after each item, except that a comma is still used between article or amendment number and section number.

Court Cases

Documentation abbreviates heavily and avoids underlining. Examples:

Doe v. State, 6 Ill. 560 (Ill. Super. Ct. 1977).

Smith v. Smith, 450 U.S. 600 (U.S. Supreme Ct. 1977).

The number before U.S. or the state (abbreviated) is the volume number; the number after the state or U.S. is the page number. "Super." is an abbreviation of "Superior" and "Ct.," of course, abbreviates "Court."

Bibliography form retains the page number(s) and is otherwise standard, with the deciding court in the position of "publisher":

Doe v. State. 6 Ill. 560. Ill. Super. Ct. 1977.

For more detailed information (which you should need only if you are specializing), the standard text is *A Uniform System of Citation,* published by the Harvard Law Review Association; a new edition (the 12th) was published in 1976.

Diaries

See "Interviews."

Dictionaries

In citing dictionaries and encyclopedias, it is important to specify the edition (other than the first) because there are likely to be extensive text changes from one edition to the next. Example:

Webster's Third New International Dictionary, 2d ed. (1967).

Note that you omit the word defined and the page number, and that you do not underline the title of the dictionary.

Dissertations (Ph.D.)

Although most dissertations and Master's theses are book length, their titles are in quotation marks instead of underscored, because they are unpublished. Example:

John Doe, "Mirages in California, 1960–1975" (Ph.D. diss., New York University, 1977), p. 23.

Editors

When citing a note, introduction, or preface written by an editor or annotator other than the original author, give the editor's name first in the footnote:

Theodor H. Gaster, ed., *The New Golden Bough,* by James George Frazer (New York: Criterion, 1959), p. 390n.

The "n" stands for "note." The *bibliography* entry would be under "Frazer."

Interviews

The form is: interviewee, detailed information, place, date. Example:

John Doe, optometrist, personal interview on mirages, Cambridge, Mass., July 4, 1978.

If you taped the interview, substitute the word *taped* for the word *personal.*
In the *bibliography,* the form would be:

John Doe, optometrist. Personal interview on mirages. Cambridge, Mass., July 4, 1978.

For *letters* or *diaries,* use the same form, substituting as follows:

John Doe to Jane Smith, Letter, July 4, 1978.

John Doe, Diary, July 1928–Sept. 1978, entry for July 4, 1978.

In the *bibliography,* put periods after the names and after "Letter" and "Diary."

Lectures

The form is: lecturer, title of the lecture (if there is one), detailed information, place, date. Example:

John Doe, "Mirages," Lecture at Young Men's Hebrew Association, New York, N.Y., Oct. 16, 1977.

In the *bibliography*, substitute periods for the commas after " 'Mirages,' " and after "Association."

Legal Documents

Public laws, private laws, joint Congressional resolutions, concurring Congressional resolutions, Presidential proclamations, and U.S. treaties are published annually in *Statutes At Large.* In addition, the *United States Code Congressional and Administrative News,* listed by Congress and Session numbers, and found in the political science reference area in many libraries, gives public laws, proclamations, executive orders, and also legislative histories of laws. Many libraries also have "slip laws" files, usually in the political science reference area. These files contain, in pamphlet form, individual laws too new to be bound into *Statutes At Large.*

The footnote form for Congressional resolutions and Presidential proclamations is the same as for *government documents* (see Figure 11). The form for public and private laws is:

Title, Statutes At Large, vol. number, Public [or Private] Law number, page number (date).

Example:

An Act to Protect the Rights of Children, Statutes At Large, 92, Pub. L. 81-16, 45 (1977).

The only difference for *bibliography* form is that a period, not a comma, is put after the title of the law.

Letters

See "Interviews."

Manuscript Collections

Give location of collection, title of collection, and number or other designation of the part you used. Example:

American Museum, Doe MSS, 403, fol. 66b.

(MSS=manuscript; fol.=folio.)
A *bibliography* entry would read:

American Museum. Doe MSS.

Minutes

If possible, identify the author(s) of committee analyses. Example:

John Doe, Secretary, Minutes of the Roosevelt University Faculty Senate, Roosevelt University, Chicago, Ill., Oct. 12, 1977.

The *bibliography* form is:

Roosevelt University, Chicago, Ill., Faculty Senate, Minutes of the Meeting of Oct. 12, 1977, by John Doe, Secretary.

Motion Pictures

Because motion pictures are relatively new sources for study, there is little agreement on their footnote and bibliography forms. Literally, they should not be listed in a bibliography, which is "a list of books," but should be separately itemized in a "filmography." Film books or journals do this, but if you use only a few films as sources for a paper with another focus, include the films alphabetically in your bibliography.

As with other forms of citation, the principle for motion picture citation is to give all relevant, helpful reference information. In *footnoting*, the key information is title and date of release. But it is almost always more natural to include that information, and any other information that is pertinent, such as producer, players, director, in the body of your text, rather than in a footnote.

In your *bibliography or filmography*, give the film title first. This suggestion is based on the esthetic principle that a motion picture is the corporate creative work of a "company" of individuals. *The MLA Handbook*, on the other hand, gives the director's name first, reflecting the theory that the director is the major creator, or "author" of a film. You will have to judge if the director, or the company of producer-director-writers-actors is "author." Generally, the following form will apply: After the title, give pertinent information and list the creators who are relevant to your subject. (For example, an international film study should name the movie's country of origin.) Major creators are producers, directors, writers, and performers. But, for example, a science fiction filmography might well include the special effects creators and the designers.

Here are examples of filmography entries that emphasize different information about the films cited:

Bergman, Ingmar. *The Seventh Seal.* Sweden. 1956.

An Unmarried Woman. Written and directed by Paul Mazursky, starring Jill Clayburgh, Alan Bates, Michael Murphy, and Cliff Gorman. 1978.

The first entry lists the writer-director, Bergman, in the position of "author"; the second emphasizes the film as a company, or joint production of its writer-director and leading players.

If you are citing the published screenplay of a film, use book form, giving author's name first. For example (if footnote form):

Joan Tewkesbury, *Nashville: An original screenplay* (New York: Bantam Books, 1976), n. pag.

Pamphlets

Use the same form as for books.

Plays

Plays are footnoted like books, but if they have act and scene numbers, these are added in parenthesis after the page number(s) of the edition you used. The act and scene numbers are helpful for someone who is using a different edition.

Give acts in capital Roman numerals; scenes in small Roman numerals; and lines, if the play has them, in Arabic numerals. Examples:

> William Shakespeare, *The Tragedy of King Lear,* ed. Russell Fraser, *The Signet Classic Shakespeare,* ed. Sylvan Barnet (New York: New American Library, 1963), p. 58 (IV.i.86).

Note that no spaces are left after the periods following act and scene numbers.

> Tennessee Williams, *The Night of the Iguana* (New York: Signet Books, 1964), p. 115 (III).

> Aeschylus, *Agamemnon,* I, trans. Richmond Lattimore, *The Complete Greek Tragedies,* ed. David Grene and Richmond Lattimore (Chicago: The University of Chicago Press, 1959), 35:20.

Agamemnon has no act and scene divisions; 36 is the page number; 20 is the line number in this edition. The abbreviation "p." is not used for "page" when reference is to a volume in a series, as *The Complete Greek Tragedies.*

Recordings

As with motion pictures and television and radio programs, the principle is to give the information that is relevant to your purpose, beginning with the most important item for your purpose: the performer, composer, lyricist, or whoever. For example:

> Antonio Barbosa, *Chopin Waltzes,* Connoisseur Society Recording CS-2036, 1971.

Frequently, a date will not be given for a recording. The recording number (in this case, CS-2036), is important in helping your reader locate the record. Note that the title of the record is underscored, not enclosed within quotation marks; if your reference is to a *part*— for example, a song—of the record, that part should be in quotation marks and the name of the record underscored.

If you are citing the liner notes on a record, include "liner notes" or "jacket notes" and the name of their author, if it is given:

> Richard Freed, liner notes to Antonio Barbosa, *Chopin Waltzes,* Connoisseur Society Recording CS-2036, 1971.

Television and Radio Programs

As with motion pictures, instructions vary on what to include in footnotes and bibliography and in what order. In addition, television and radio programs are more ephemeral than motion pictures, making it more difficult for you to give your readers the information they might want on your sources.

As with film, the principle is to give the primary information first—the source of production and date of performance—and then as much other information as is pertinent to your purpose. Examples:

> See It Now, CBS, Jan. 4, 1955: "A Conversation with J. Robert Oppenheimer," narrator, Edward R. Murrow.

> ABC, June 9, 1977: "Fidel Castro Speaks," interviewer, Barbara Walters.

Note that the series title comes first if there is one (such as *See It Now*), and that it is underscored, like a magazine title.

If you know that the performance date you are citing is not the date of original broadcast, note in parenthesis "repeat" or "delayed broadcast":

> *The Dick Van Dyke Show,* WGN-TV Chicago, Sept. 12, 1977 (repeat broadcast).

If the date of original broadcast is pertinent to your subject, make every effort to get it and include it in your text, footnotes, and bibliography. Put a semicolon after "broadcast," write "originally broadcast," and then give the date.

If your text has focused on the writing or directing of the program cited, on the performers, or on any other creator, list their titles and names in series, separated by commas, following the parenthesis "(repeat broadcast)." Similarly, if it is pertinent, follow "narrator, Edward R. Murrow" and "interviewer, Barbara Walters," with the titles and names of producers, directors, writers, editors, special effects personnel, and the like.

Theses (Master's)

See Dissertations.

FINISHING THE PAPER:
REWRITING AND PROOFREADING

GENERAL GUIDELINES

All too often we work up to our final deadlines, without allowing time for rewriting our papers—that is, taking our first draft and writing a second or even third draft, if necessary—and not allowing time for proofreading. This error in work scheduling is costly and frustrating. So, when planning your overall work schedule for invention, research, development, writing, leave sufficient time for revision and proofreading. You will need time to do at least a second draft; then, if your second draft needs only minor revision, you can type the final paper.

Perhaps the best aid to successful revision and proofreading is a friend—someone who will read your paper or listen to you read it aloud and help you catch omissions and errors in content, organiztion, and mechanics (such as spelling). Another person's reactions can be very helpful. Through them you can test your arguments; uncover your hidden assumptions; and learn where you need to rearrange the order in which you have presented your material, define more, give more examples, make your generalizations clearer, eliminate the hostility from your tone (or the cuteness, sarcasm, slanginess), and so on. In short, with the help of a listener or reader, you can better test all the many checkpoints at which you, the writer, interface with your audience.

If you have to work alone, it is a good idea to first take a day off, if you can, and then read the paper aloud to yourself—that is, to your other, critic-self. Reading aloud is perhaps the most successful technique for catching spelling errors, omitted words, and other "typos"; for hearing any -s or -ed endings you omitted from verbs or nouns; for hearing the sentence fragment that doesn't work, the run-on sentence, the pronoun that is plural but refers to a singular noun (or vice-versa), the modifying clause that is misplaced from the words it modifies, the verb predicate that is singular though its subject is plural (or vice-versa), and other common mistakes in grammar.

Finally, take the time for a last, solitary engagement with your paper. This will be your last chance to make it say what you want to say and look the way you want it to look. Looks do count, and your best work deserves to look good. (If you can use correction fluid neatly, use it to white-out typos; otherwise, cross out and ink in corrections neatly.) Make sure you have followed all the instructions given you for the format of your paper; if you haven't, or if you have too many corrections in your final paper, it will probably not be taken as final but rather as a "work in progress." For this last run-through, have on hand, and use, the dictionary, your texts on grammar and this text, your earlier drafts, all your note cards, and as many of your sources as possible (what if you find you have left out a word in copying a quotation or forgotten to include in your footnote the page number referred to?). And remember, as you put the finishing touches to it, that although you may feel that you never want to hear of your subject or see your paper again, you really do care about it. It is your creation.

THE TITLE

But wait—you probably forgot the title! It is the last thing almost everyone writes (although those rare people who develop a title early in their inventing process are helped in keeping to their purpose.)

To develop a title, look at the statement of purpose or problem in your introduction. Look at the main headings in your outline. Think carefully about how to convey succinctly what your subject is and what you do with it (analyze it, give its history, compare it to something else, and the like). For example, consider the difference between a title such as "African Masks" and "African Masks: The True Faces of a Society." This longer title reflects the writer's overall point—that African masks are not peripheral or merely decorative, but reflect and reveal the values and mores of the societies that create them.

If you have a special audience or purpose in mind, try to convey that in your title. For example, "A Manager's Guide to Women Employees" suggests a special audience (office managers), and through the word *guide,* a practical purpose. In brief, the title is your first chance to establish your credibility and to capture the interest of your audience.

The remaining sections of this chapter are a checklist to test your drafts and your final paper, key parts of a sample college research paper, and a glossary of abbreviations used in footnoting.

CHECKLIST FOR FINISHING AND
PROOFREADING PAPERS

This checklist is in four parts: (A) content and organization; (B) usage, mechanics, and punctuation; (C) format; and (D) footnotes and bibliography.

A. Content and Organization

    1. Does the paper fulfill the purpose—solve the problem—it stated in its opening? That is, does it seem that the *purpose* of your *subject* will convince your *audience?*

    2. Are your most important points emphasized—for example, by being placed at the end or the beginning of your paper and your paragraphs? Are you as a reader persuaded?

    3. Are your generalizations supported by specific evidence?

4. Are your paragraphs topically contained units? Are the topics, or central ideas, clearly stated? Are the paragraphs developed enough (are they too short)? Are they focused on only one topic, or on several unified or closely related small topics (that is, if they don't seem focused, are they too long; do they ramble)?

5. Is your quoted or paraphrased matter excessive? That is, does the paper deemphasize your ideas by overusing source material? (Here an outsider can be particularly helpful—we all have a tendency to overuse source material because we worked so long and hard to research it.)

6. Are there logical transitions between paragraphs, and between sentences within each paragraph? Repetition of key words and ideas can be helpful, as well as the sparing use of appropriate transitional "markers," such as *but, in addition, consequently, nevertheless, however,* and the like.

7. Does your conclusion satisfy you that your purpose has been achieved?

8. Check your sentences for *style*: Are there too many very short sentences? Does the paper *sound* abrupt or choppy? Are any sentences so long—that is, have so many modifying phrases and clauses—that they may be confusing? Do your pronouns refer clearly to nouns? (If you hear too many pronouns, the answer to this question is probably "no.") Are series of phrases or clauses in your sentences parallel in grammatical form? Do you use active verbs and the personal voice wherever they are appropriate? ("I discovered why the machine failed," communicates more directly than, "The reasons that the machine failed were discovered.")

9. Are there unnecessary repetitions of ideas or words? That is, are you in control, or are you belaboring an idea because you are unsure that you made your point?

10. Do any of your points seem underdeveloped? Where should they be developed?

11. Are there any statements in the paper that you think will antagonize your audience?

Check the following items that are applicable to your paper:

12. Does your analysis, or breakdown of your subject into its parts, hold up? Are all the parts of the subject developed? If any are omitted or deemphasized, do you justify what you have done?

13. Does your classification of the parts of your subject hold up? Are the parts all members of that set? Are there any other members of the set, or class, that you have omitted? If so, do you justify it?

14. Is your least-to-most important order logically consistent? In your most-to-least order, do you restate the most important item in the conclusion? Is your simple-to-complex order logically consistent?

15. Is your spatial order clear? Are any items out of place?

16. Are any items in your chronological order out of sequence? If so, do you justify the organization?

17. Are your causes clearly related to your effects as necessary, sufficient, or contributory? Are removed causes justified?

18. Are parallel or contrasting points equally developed? If one is more developed than another, do you justify your emphasis?

19. Do your analogies or dialectics represent logical, understandable relationships?

20. Is your paper's problem stated clearly? If it is not explicit, do you clearly *imply* your subject and what your audience should know about it?

21. Do you qualify the limits, or scope, of your paper or any of its parts that need to be qualified?

22. Do you define unfamiliar or controversial concepts? In your definition, do you use examples? Describe function? Compare or contrast the term or concept being defined to relevant, known terms? Do you use the history or etymology of the meaning of the term?

23. Is your content or arrangement unusual or potentially unclear, so that you should explain your material or organization at the beginning of the paper? If so, have you justified your unusual content or organization?

B. Usage, Mechanics, and Punctuation

These are checks on only the most common problems in usage, mechanics, and punctuation. Consult your grammar text on these and others for more detailed help.

1. Is your usage of vocabulary, parts of speech, and punctuation "standard English"? If not, do you justify it to your audience?

2. Are your sentences complete?
   a. Do any lack subject, predicate, or object or complement— that is, are any fragments? If so, can you justify the fragment stylistically?
   b. Do you have run-on or fused sentences, which should be two (or more) sentences?
   c. Have you put a comma between two complete sentences, instead of a period or semicolon?

3. Do your subjects and verbs agree in tense and person?
   a. Does the verb reflect the past when it should? (Especially check for the -ed ending.)
   b. Is the verb plural when the subject is, and singular when the subject is (for example, "Mary goes," not "Mary go")?
   c. Are verb tenses consistent; for example, do you avoid switching back and forth between past and present?

4. Do your nouns used as possessives appear in the possessive form (for example, "Mary's room," not "Marys room" or "Mary room")?

5. Do your pronouns have antecedents—that is, nouns they clearly refer to (for example, is the plural "group" followed by the plural pronoun "they")?

6. Are your modifying clauses, phrases, or words placed so that they refer clearly to what they modify? "The woman seems old in green" means one thing, and "The woman in green seems old" means something else.

7. Words:
   a. Are all spelled correctly?
   b. Is each the word that most accurately expresses your idea? Do any words seem to be repeated too often? (Where you have doubts, go to the dictionary or Roget's *Thesaurus* of synonyms and variants for help.)

8. Period, comma, semicolon: Do not use the comma between sentences; use period, or the semicolon if the two sentences are very closely related (note the use of the semicolon in this sentence). Use the colon, not the semicolon, to introduce material that expands on what you have just written ("The following attended: Rossiter, Rossi, and Ross").

9. Apostrophe: Use it to indicate a possessive noun ("John's") and a contraction ("it's," for "it is").

10. Hyphen: Are words divided at the ends of lines according to their syllables? (If in doubt, check the dictionary.) Don't use the hyphen (-) where you should use the dash (–); that is, to set off and emphasize part of your sentence ("Of the three who came—Rossiter, Rossi, and Ross—only Ross was sober").

11. Capitals: Capitalize the first letter in a sentence, proper names, titles of works of art or texts, and people's titles when they are followed by the person's name. (Except in the case of presidents, the title is not capitalized when it is not followed by a name—that is, "Dr. Jones," but not, "The Doctor said. . . .")

12. Underscoring and quotation marks: Underscore in the text all titles that are underscored in footnotes, such as books,

magazines, and works of art. Use quotation marks for the titles of poems, magazine or newspaper articles, and other titles that appear in quotation marks in footnotes. You can also underscore any words in your text that you want to emphasize, but use this (like the exclamation point) sparingly.

C. Format

In some cases you will be required to conform to a standard format. If you have not been given a format, here are the general standards:

1. Size of paper: Use white 8½ x 11-inch paper, or if you are handwriting, paper of the same size that is lined.

2. Margins: Use 1-inch margins, except on the top and the left, binding margin. Leave 1½ inches here.

3. Typing: Make every effort to type, or have your paper typed. If you handwrite, write legibly in blue or black in. On either typed or handwritten papers, use only one side of the paper and double space so your reader can comment.

4. Title page: Either make a separate page on which you center the title of your paper, your name, the date, and for whom or what the paper has been written; or leave a 2-inch margin at the top of the first page of your paper, then give the title, and so on, centered, and leave about 2 inches below the first line of your text.

5. Footnote placement: Either list footnotes on a separate page(s) at the end of your paper or put them at the bottom of the page they appear on. Review pages 129–130 for the mechanics of footnote placement, and see Section D below.

6. Bibliography: Bibliographies are placed last in a paper. See Section D.2.d. below.

7. Binding: A staple in the upper lefthand corner secures the pages and allows easy turning of the pages; avoid fancy bindings.

D. Footnotes and Bibliography

1. Treatment of sources in your paper:
   a. Check your quotations and paraphrases: should any paraphrases be quotations instead? Are the words you have quoted special enough that you should not paraphrase?
      i. Do your quotes describe things that are complicated, unusual, or controversial? If not, consider paraphrasing.
      ii. Are your paraphrases fair to your sources? Do they keep —that is, quote—key terms, or substitute indisputable synonyms? Do you preserve all the meaning of what you paraphrase?
      iii. Have you footnoted your paraphrases as well as your quotations?
   b. Have you made every effort to use original sources, rather than a source that quotes or paraphrases the original source?
   c. Have you footnoted (i) all quotations, (ii) all ideas not your own, (iii) little known facts, and (iv) lengthy factual matter drawn from a source or sources, such as the history or background of your subject?
   d. Do you refer to your sources within your text; that is, does your text introduce a quotation or paraphrase by citing the source—for example, "According to Freud"—or does your reader have to find the source in the footnote?
   e. Are your long quotations (four or more lines) in proper form: indented, single-spaced, and not enclosed by quotation marks?
   f. If you omit words from your quotation, do you use the ellipsis?
   g. If you add to a quotation, is your addition enclosed in brackets?
   h. Have you (i) put the footnote number at the end of each quotation or paraphrase—superscript (^{22}) and (ii) numbered footnotes consecutively throughout your paper? (iii) Have you left two spaces between each footnote? (iv) If you have positioned your footnotes at the bottom of each page, have you left two spaces below the text and then drawn a line, 1 1/2" long from the left margin, to separate the text from the footnotes?

2. Sources in footnotes and bibliography:

a. Whether at the end of each page, or at the end of the paper, is each footnote indented 5 spaces on its first line, single-spaced, and separated from the next footnote by a double space?

b. Does each footnote have all the necessary information in the correct sequence, according to the footnote diagrams?

c. Could you use any of your footnotes to give additional information or comment? On the other hand, does any of the material in your "comment footnotes" really belong in your text?

d. Does your bibliography have the form it should have according to the bibliography diagram? Have you listed all (and only) works that are directly related to your subject? Would it be helpful to your reader to annotate the bibliography—that is, to summarize the content and value of each entry? (Unless you have done this in your text, the answer to this question is "yes.")

e. Do the irregular entries in your footnotes or bibliography follow the corresponding examples given for irregular entries on pages 145-154?

f. If your instructor has requested that you use a special form for your footnotes or bibliography, have you followed this form?

SAMPLE RESEARCH PAPER *

Following are four sample pages from a research paper: a first page, an inner page, a footnote page and a bibliography page. On the page facing the first page and the inner page, we have noted some of the important points about writing research papers illustrated in each sample.

---

* We thank Rosalyn Grennan for permission to use this paper, written at Roosevelt University in April 1978.

SAMPLE FIRST PAGE

TELLING LEFT FROM RIGHT:

1   A Description and Analysis of the Cerebral Laterality Theory

2   Perhaps no other physiological element of the experience of being human has evoked more curiosity among humans than the brain and all its workings. From professional journal to popular periodical, the literature of brain research and theory occupies the printed page and invites the continuing interest of the human mind, which, in such speculations, is actually probing the physical source

3 of its own existence. The purpose of this paper is to investigate one such hypothesis; namely, the cerebral laterality theory, i.e., the "right-left brain theory," by 1) defining its tenets, 2) elaborating on the conditions and difficulties surrounding the research, and 3) citing the evidence in support of the theory.

4   Among the various hypotheses of brain function the cerebral laterality theory, in particular, has provoked much exploration and merits our discussion. In the last few years numerous articles have appeared in the press describing a theory of brain function which correlates various behaviors with either the left or right cerebral

5 hemisphere. An article in Playboy magazine (attesting to the popular interest in this subject) gave this simple explanation to the layperson:

6   . . . the right and left hemispheres of the brain have different functions. . . . The left hemisphere seems to be concerned with speech, reading, writing, naming, the perception of significant order and mathematical functions. It is worldly, analytical, logical. The right hemisphere seems to be concerned with spatial relations, music, emotion, facial recognition and perception of abstract patterns. It is intuitive, symbolic, holistic and simultaneous. In short, left side logical, right side creative. . . .[1]

COMMENT ON SAMPLE FIRST PAGE

1 Subtitle clarifies title and provides a more detailed description of what the paper is about.

2 In first paragraph, the author establishes the significance of her topic by relating it to an issue of general interest.

3 The author provides a clear statement of purpose, which also defines a difficult term that is important to her topic, and tells the reader what to expect in the rest of the paper.

4 The author provides a brief overview of articles on the topic to further establish its currency.

5 Reference to *Playboy* incorporates some footnote information into the text, providing a context for her quotation and further illustrating her point about the popularity of the topic.

6 Long quotation indented and single spaced also illustrates use of ellipses in editing quoted material to remove that which is irrelevant.

SAMPLE INNER PAGE

1   Besides the formidable physical nature of the subject of our research, the experimentation itself presents problems, mostly with the
idea of the control group, a principle that is fundamentally manda-
2 tory to empirical research. Although electroencephalogram (EEG)
readings -- electrode stimulation of various parts of the brain to map
its functions -- have been done on healthy subjects,[6] the great body
of basic information has been acquired through work with epileptic
and brain lesion patients.[7] In addition, the observations subsequent
to treatment of these patients were in many cases made by medical
personnel not trained in psychology. One might question their use
of psychological terms to describe behavior; their objectivity might
3 also be subject to doubt.[8]
4   The validity of local electrode stimulation as a way of mapping
brain function is suspect, due to some inconsistency in duplicating
results.[9] One example presents itself in recent work with EEG
readings from the implantation of large numbers of electrodes in
cats' brains: The results point in a direction away from the concept
5 of localization of function. In these experiments a cat was shown a
flashing light and electrical waves were picked up of the same fre-
6 quency as the light. The frequency was called the "labeled rhythm."
When cats previously conditioned to respond to this light in various
7 ways (such as jumping) were implanted with electrodes, the labeled
rhythm was observed to spread from visual brain areas to many other
areas.[10]

COMMENT ON SAMPLE INNER PAGE

1 Note that in this paragraph, the author makes a number of critical judgments about the evidence she is presenting.

2 This sentence illustrates paraphrasing of sources as well as the placement of footnotes, both within a sentence and at the end of the sentence.

3 Footnote 8 is ambiguous. Is the "doubt" on the part of the author of the paper, or on the part of the source cited in the footnote?

4 By repeating the phrase "electrode stimulation" from the previous paragraph, the author establishes a clear connection between the two paragraphs.

5 A specific example is used to support the general statement made at the beginning of this paragraph.

6 The first use of the specialized term "labeled rhythm" is placed in quotation marks to indicate the term has a particular meaning in this research.

Now that she has established the use of the term "labeled rhythm," the author drops the quotation marks.

SAMPLE FOOTNOTE PAGE

FOOTNOTES

[1]John Lobell, "Eureka! I'm Coming." Playboy, February, 1978, p. 137.

[2]Hugh Brown, Brain and Behavior: A Textbook of Physiological Psychology (New York: Oxford University Press, 1976), p. 24.

[3]Ibid., p. 25.

[4]A. R. Luria, The Working Brain: An Introduction to Neuropsychology, trans. Basil Haigh (New York: Basic Books, 1973), p. 31.

[5]Keith Oatley, Brain Mechanism and Mind (New York: Dutton, 1972), p. 8.

[6]E. R. John, "How the Brain Works -- A New Theory?" Psychology Today, October, 1976, p. 48.

[7]Luria, p. 9.

[8]Elliot S. Valenstein, Brain Control: A Critical Examination of Brain Stimulation and Psychosurgery (New York: Wiley, 1973), p. 35.

[9]Ibid., p. 97.

[10]John, p. 29.

[11]Michael C. Corballis and Ivan L. Beale, The Psychology of Left and Right (New Jersey: Lawrence Erlbaum Associates, 1976), p. 95.

[12]R. J. Trotter, "Other Hemisphere," Science News, April 3, 1976, p. 219.

[13]Wilder Penfield, The Mystery of the Mind: A Critical Study of Consciousness and the Human Brain (Princeton: Princeton University Press, 1975), p. XXV.

[14]Hugh Brown, Brain and Behavior: A Textbook of Physiological Psychology (New York: Oxford University Press, 1976), p. 313.

[15]Ibid., p. 315.

[16]Ibid., pp. 316–318.

[17]Penfield, p. 4.

[18]"Brain Asymmetry Present at Birth," Science News, October 30, 1976, p. 277.

[19]G. H. Yeni-Komshiam and D. A. Benson, "Anatomical Study of Cerebral Asymmetry in the Temporal Lobe of Humans, Chimpanzees and Rhesus Monkeys," Science, April 23, 1976, p. 389.

SAMPLE BIBLIOGRAPHY PAGE

BIBLIOGRAPHY

Bener, T. G. and Chiarello, R. J. "Cerebral Dominance in Musicians and Non-musicians," Science, July 4, 1975, pp. 68–69.

Brown, Hugh. Brain and Behavior: A Textbook of Physiological Psychology. New York: Oxford University Press, 1976.

Corballis, Michael C. and Beale, Ivan, L. The Psychology of Left and Right. New Jersey: Lawrence Erlbaum Associates, 1976.

Goleman, Daniel. "J. B.'s Startling Recovery," Psychology Today, May, 1976, p. 51.

Hecaln, Henry and de Ajuriaguerra, Julian. Left-handedness: Manual Superiority and Cerebral Dominance. Translated by Eric Ponda. New York: Grune & Stratton, 1964.

Horn, Jack. "Good Managers Rely on Their Right Brains," Psychology Today, October, 1976, p. 36.

Horn, Jack. "The Hand is Faster Than the Eye, Especially if You Read Backwards," Psychology Today, November, 1977, pp. 130-131.

John, E. R. "How the Brain Works -- A New Theory?" Psychology Today, May, 1976, pp. 48-49.

Lewin, Roger. Hormones: Chemical Communicators. New York: Anchor Books, 1973.

Lobell, John. "Eureka! I'm Coming," Playboy, February, 1978, pp. 137-138.

Luria, A. R. The Working Brain: An Introduction to Neuropsychology. Translated by Basil Haigh. New York: Basic Books, 1973.

Oatley, Keith, Brain Mechanism and Mind. New York: Dutton, 1972.

Olson, Don A. "Crisis: Reactions to the Disability," from Lecture at the Rehabilitation Institute, Chicago, September 24, 1975.

Penfield, Wilder. The Mystery of the Mind: A Critical Study of Consciousness and the Human Brain. Princeton: Princeton University Press, 1975.

Schwartz, G. C., et al. "Right Hemisphere Lateralization for Emotion in the Human Brain: Interactions with Cognition," Science, October 17, 1975, pp. 286–288.

Trotter, R. J. "Other Hemisphere," Science News, April 3, 1976, pp. 218–220.

GLOSSARY OF ABBREVIATIONS COMMONLY USED IN FOOTNOTING

anon.: anonymous.

ca., c.: circa: about; used to indicate approximate dates. Underscore.

ch., chs.: chapter, chapters.

col., cols.: column, columns.

diss.: Ph. D. dissertation.

ed., eds.: edition, editor, editors.

e.g.: exempli gratia: for example.

et al.: et alii: and others.

fig., figs.: figure, figures.

fol.: folio.

ibid.: ibidem: in the same place; used to refer to the footnote directly preceding. Using the author's name is clearer.

i.e.: id est: that is (in clarification).

introd.: introduction, introduced by.

l., ll.: line, lines (as in plays).

loc. cit.: loco citato: in the place cited (earlier, before intervening citations). Avoid; use author's name and title, if you use more than one work by the author. Underscore.

ms, mss: manuscript, manuscripts. Use a period after when referring to a specific manuscript.

n.d.: no date given.

no., nos.: number, numbers.

n.p.: no place of publication given.

n. pag.: no pagination in text.

op. cit.: opere citato: in the work cited; used in reference to a work recently cited, but on different pages. As with *loc. cit.,* avoid, and use the author's name and, if necessary, title. Underscore

p., pp.: page, pages. Omit when there is a volume number.

pl., pls.: plate, plates.

pref.: preface.

rev.: revised; review (as in articles which are reviews of books).

rpt.: reprinted.

sc.: scene.

sec., secs.: section, sections.

sic: source's quote is erroneous in content or grammar. Underscore.

trans.: translator, translated, translation.

vol., vols.: volume, volumes; do not use abbreviation when page number is also given—in this case, use only numbers (volume and page); i.e., use abbreviation mainly in bibliography, not footnotes.

vs.: versus: against; v. is used in legal citations.

INDEX